Insights in Space

How to use Clean Space to solve problems, generate ideas and spark creativity

James Lawley and **Marian Way**

CLEAN PUBLISHING

Insights in Space

How to use Clean Space to solve problems,
generate ideas and spark creativity

by James Lawley and Marian Way

Published by Clean Publishing

14 Anson Grove,

Portchester, Fareham

Hants PO16 8JG

Printed in Great Britain by Cedar Group

Illustrations by Lyneth Howells-Snoddon

ISBN: 978-0-9574866-2-1

Post-it Note is trademark of 3M.

For Penny and John

At the edge between the known and the unknown there is a fertile place, full of possibility. Playing at the edge can lead us to experience fresh new learning, creativity, joy and wonder.

STEVEN D'SOUZA AND DIANA RENNER

Acknowledgements

First and foremost, we are indebted to David Grove, without whom Clean Space, or indeed any clean approach, would not exist. It was David's extensive exploration of language, metaphor, space and networks that led him to invent this exquisitely simple and innovative facilitation process.

While Clean Space would not exist without David, this book would not have been brought into being without the incredible support we've received from our respective spouses, Penny Tompkins and John Way. As well as providing a copious supply of meals, drinks and feedback, they've also accompanied us on our writing retreats, sharing the kitchen and indulging in a spot of fishing while we've been talking, mapping our ideas and writing together. And then making sure we got out and had some fun as well.

Caitlin Walker and Shaun Hotchkiss have also been wonderfully supportive, providing their home as a venue for our first joint Clean Space workshop, letting other projects take a back seat in order for this one to have the attention it needed, and supplying helpful feedback.

Thanks are also due to Lyneth Howells-Snoddon, whose delightful illustrations have helped our text come alive – and who continued with the project even when her illustrating hand was damaged.

Many of our colleagues in the clean community have shared their stories, examples and transcripts or feature in some way in this book. Thank you to: Albéric Augeard, Chris de Graal, Jackie Lawlor, Jeni Edge, John Martin, Judy Rees, Ken Smith, Lynne Burney, Maaike Nooitgedagt, Phil Swallow, Sarah Wilson, Sue Charman, Wendy Nieuwland and all those who wished to remain anonymous (we have changed some names in the book for this reason).

Last, and most definitely not least, we owe a massive debt of gratitude to everyone who read the book at various stages and gave us feedback along with excellent suggestions for improvement: Annemeik van Helsdingen, Bev Martin, Caitlin Walker, Charles Faulkner, Charlotte Ellis, Gina Campbell, Jonathan Way, Kate Smith, Kathy Brown, Penny Tompkins, Rachel Hankins, Sue Charman, Sue Sharp and Tamsin Hartley.

Table of Contents

Chapter 3: How to Run the Process

Chapter 4: Navigating Towards Creativity

Chapter 5: Conditional Questions and Directions

Chapter 6: Getting Creative with Clean Space

Chapter 7: Group Clean Space

Chapter 8: And What Difference Does Knowing All This Make?

Foreword

Current Social Psychology, which includes Behavioral Economics, delights in pointing out how 'irrationally rational' we all are. One reason often given for this is all of us are stuck in a 'situated perspective' in everyday English, our own personal point-of-view. The conventional solution for this is to exchange our 'inside view' for an outside one – a switch from subject to observer. There are, in fact, many more options than that. In this book James Lawley and Marian Way guide you in how to naturally create multiple perspectives that inform each other and then become a new and emergent network of possibilities that were not even initially imagined.

This book is a learning, practicing and teaching toolkit methodically organized in its presentation, selection of examples and sequence of increasingly customized processes. Being about 'space', it is gratifying to see it so clearly and effectively illustrated. Its beginning-to-end emphasis on applications will surely please its intended audience. Yet this does not illuminate the sophisticated communications insights that make them possible, so let's do that here.

The Clean Space process starts with 'externalizing' the explorer's experience of their desired outcome or topic of interest. With this simple perceptual shift, the topic of interest is 'in the world' instead of 'being the world', thus overcoming a Behavioral Economics bias – the Illusion of Objectivity. Known in philosophy and developmental psychology as Naïve Realism, it is our ubiquitous inability to separate our ideas about the world from our perception of the world. Through this perspective shift, we can become clearer about the difference.

Next, the explorer is invited to find another space. A change in space necessarily involves a physical perspective shift, and with it, a shift in mental space. This new and different physical and mental space might be the perspective of a younger or older self, or another person's point-of-view (which may also be from another time) or something else entirely. These perspective shifts parallel how with our binocular vision we create depth perception. Our ability to see – physically and mentally – into situations is enhanced.

When a third space is added, the usually invisible and significant influence of each space's situation (context) becomes self-evident. Outside of our awareness, each situation frames the meaning of the thoughts, actions and emotions we have within it, and so sets limits on what we 'see'. As additional spaces are added, the range of possible context perspectives multiplies and with them the potential possibilities. This is another major perspective shift.

After exploring several spaces, the explorer is encouraged to establish links between these spaces. This is intentionally engaging a natural process. All of our experiences have their existing linkages – technically know as 'reentrant circuits'. This is how we get from one thought to another, hold our memories together, have beliefs and so much more. The process of inviting links among the selected spaces serves these same purposes: vivifying their new and emergent meanings, creating cascades of new insights and securing their interconnections.

Clean Space is a significant contribution to our understanding of how the language of everyday metaphors and mental spaces organize and impart meaning to our life experiences, showing us how to use them to effectively facilitate change in individuals, groups and organizations. *Insights in Space: How to use Clean Space to solve problems, generate ideas and spark creativity* is an excellent introduction to this work.

Charles Faulkner
May 2017

*Trust yourself. You know more
than you think you do.*

BENJAMIN SPOCK

Preface

James's Story

I first saw David Grove demonstrate his clean approach at a seminar in 1993. He worked with two volunteer clients simultaneously, asking one client a few questions before turning to the other, going back and forth between them. I was bemused and enthralled. I had never heard of Clean Language nor seen anything like it before. I had no idea what was going on but I could sense that something extraordinary was happening.

Eighteen months were to pass before I had a chance to observe David at work again and to experience him asking *me* those unfamiliar questions. I still had no idea what he was doing but Penny Tompkins and I just knew we had to find out, and the best way to do that was to use the skills we had acquired from NLP (Neuro-Linguistic Programming) to model his expertise.

We thought it might take a year to model David but at that stage we hadn't realised he was a serial innovator and our modelling project was to become a lifelong quest. Penny and I wrote *Metaphors in Mind: Transformation through Symbolic Modelling* as a generalised model of David's work up to 1999. However, within two years of the book being published, David had taken a major innovative leap that took his work in a new direction.

I remember clearly the workshop in April 2002 when, for the first time in the UK, David unveiled his latest innovation: Clean Space. Surprisingly for a man who was normally so confident, he appeared a little nervous and eagerly sought our opinion. We said we first needed to try it with ourselves and others. A few weeks later David came to stay with us and almost the first thing he said was, "Well, what do you think?" to which Penny replied, "This one's got legs."

At the time no one realised the scale of the change in direction he had embarked upon. David used to say, "I chase ideas and wrestle with them." He fervently pursued this idea for the remaining six years of his life, creating a suite of processes he called Emergent Knowledge.

Many are called 'genius' but few can be as worthy of that title as David Grove. David loved etymology and the Latin root of genius is 'begat', a perfect metaphor for his knack of birthing so many practices. The 25-year span of David's work has provided a deep seam of wisdom for those who wish to mine its riches. This book is but one example.

Marian's Story

While James came to this work through direct contact with David Grove, most of my learning came from James and Penny. My first introduction to Clean Language and Symbolic Modelling was at an NLP Conference in 1999, where James was giving a talk on 'Binds and Double Binds'. I became the volunteer client and that session set the direction for a new phase in my life. I was bowled over by what I learned about myself and determined to learn how to use the skills James was demonstrating.

My first introduction to Clean Space was also with Penny and James. I was attending my third or fourth Clean Language workshop with them when on the last day they hired an enormous local hall for us to try Clean Space. The floor of the hall was covered with netball court markings and each pair of participants had half a court to work within.

Despite what I'd learned about Clean Language – itself a somewhat unusual practice with often surprising results – I can recall my amazement that day when we discovered that we could know wildly different things in different spaces. The term 'sacred space' also took on a new meaning as we learned to respect those court boundaries and keep out of our fellow participants' spaces.

Between then and now I have trained hundreds of people in Clean Language and Clean Space and have written a book of my own, *Clean Approaches for Coaches*. James gave me masses of useful feedback during the writing process, so when he asked if I'd like to write a book with him on the topic of Clean Space, I immediately said, "Yes."

We have spent many happy days together surrounded by Post-it Notes®; I think every single concept in this book, as well as a number that didn't make it, has been on a Post-it on a wall, floor or table at some point.

One of our challenges was how to do justice to a very spatial process which involves lots of moving about, within the confines of a book. We know the best way to understand Clean Space is to experience it, so overleaf you'll find a mini version to have a go with.

Grab some Post-it Notes (or pieces of paper) and do it now. This quick exercise will give you insights, both into the Clean Space process and into whatever topic you choose to consider.

Find a Space...

Get four Post-it Notes (or pieces of paper) and a pen.

On one Post-it, write or draw your desired outcome or topic of interest.

This can be anything at all. Something you want to create in your life. A problem you're grappling with. A topic you want to explore. A goal or a desired outcome. Anything that interests you.

Now place the Post-it Note where it needs to be.

Place it on the floor, a table or other surface, stick it on the wall or even on the ceiling. Take it outside or fold it up and put it in a cupboard. Put it wherever you like.

Keep hold of the three blank Post-its.

Place yourself where you are in relation to what's on the Post-it.

It's there. Where are you in relation to it? Are you in front of it or behind? To the side? At an angle? Is it higher or lower than you? What direction is it in? What's the distance between you and it?

(If your mobility is restricted, you can still do this activity – just adapt the instructions to make them work for you.)

And what do you know here?

Have a think. On the second Post-it Note, write one or two words that sum up your experience in this space.

And is there anything else you know here about that?

'That' is whatever you put on the first note. Add any new thoughts to the second note. Then use it to...

Mark the space.

Put the second Post-it where you are. This can be on the floor, wall, a chair etc. Later, we'll refer to this as 'Space 1'.

'that' = desired outcome or topic of interest

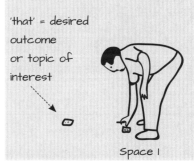

Space 1

And find another space.

Move to somewhere else – anywhere else.

And what do you know *here*?

On the third Post-it, write one or two words that sum up your experience here.

And is there anything else you know *here* about that?

'That' still refers to what you put on the first Post-it – the topic you are thinking about.

Add any additional thoughts to the third Post-it.

Mark the space.

Use the Post-it to mark the space [Space 2].

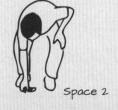

Space 2

And find another space.

And what do you know *here*?

On the remaining Post-it, write one or two words that sum up your experience here.

And is there anything else you know *here* about that?

'That' still refers to what you put on the first note – the topic you are thinking about.

Add any additional thoughts to the fourth Post-it.

Mark the space.

Use the Post-it to mark the space [Space 3].

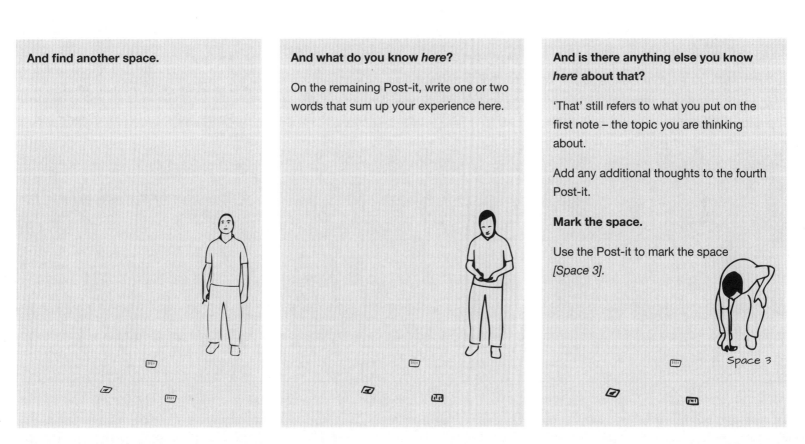

Space 3

And what do you know here about Space 1?

From where you are in Space 3, look at Space 1. What do you know?

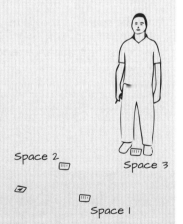

Space 2

Space 3

Space I

And what do you know here about Space 2?

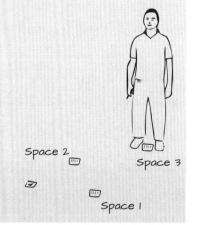

Space 2

Space 3

Space I

And return to Space 1.

And what do you know here *now*?

And what difference does knowing that make?

When you are ready, collect up your Post-it Notes.

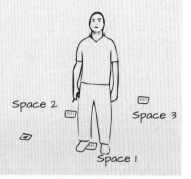

Space 2

Space 3

Space I

What Happened?

Now take some time to reflect on what you have learned from doing this activity, and what difference (if any) using space made.

What did you learn about your topic?

What was the effect of finding locations for your topic and for yourself?

How did you know when you had found each space?

Did moving from the first space to the second to the third make a difference? If so, what?

Did considering Space 1 and 2 from Space 3 add anything? If so, what?

NB. You can read about other people's experience of this activity on page 27.

We are looking to language the minimal that excites the curious.

DAVID GROVE

Introduction

Why Clean Space?

Have you ever wondered what it might be like to lay out the contents of your mind in front of you? Would considering those thoughts from a different angle or reorganising them make a difference to the way you conceive of a complex problem or a creative endeavour?

Perhaps you are already a fan of mind mapping or conceptual mapping – processes designed for getting your thoughts down onto paper and moving your ideas about until you find an arrangement that works best for you. Or maybe you have taken part in a group activity where participants put ideas onto Post-it Notes, place these on a board or wall and then organise them into categories? Or perhaps you have used the cutlery or crockery on a dinner table to explain an idea to someone, moving items around to show the relationships between various elements?

Clean Space has something in common with each of these activities in that ideas inside the mind are externalised – each given a separate space – before being related to one another and sometimes moved about. And it also has some unique features.

While it is possible to do Clean Space on your own, it is generally a facilitated process. A major benefit of having a facilitator who gives directions and asks questions is that the *explorer* (the name we are giving to the person doing the activity) does not have to think about the process and so is free to concentrate on their chosen topic.

Clean Space is also a 3D process. Instead of looking at a map on a page, Post-its on a board or items on a table, the explorer uses different locations within a room or outdoors to signify the various aspects of their topic. And once these are established the explorer

walks around their own network of ideas. This means that their *body* is involved as well as their mind. While many creative processes talk about taking multiple perspectives, they usually mean 'metaphorically speaking'. By identifying six or so spaces in a room, the explorer will literally view their topic from a number of different angles. In doing so, problems are solved, new ideas are generated and creativity is sparked.

Six angles give more perspectives.

And it is not only the body that gets involved. The explorer can also utilise the *environment* to learn more about what is going on for them, accessing information not easily available otherwise. For example, physically standing in a corner may evoke the sense of having been metaphorically 'backed into a corner'. Or the sun may start to shine and 'cast a light' on some of the explorer's spaces, leaving the others in shadow. In almost all Clean Space sessions, the space takes on extra meaning for the explorer and becomes what its inventor, counselling psychologist David Grove, called *psychoactive*. The explorer is no longer simply wandering around a room while talking about their ideas; they relate to the space as though it is imbued with symbolic information tailor-made for them.

A further feature of Clean Space is that the explorer is encouraged to create a *network* of spaces. Once the explorer identifies a number of places and discovers what he or she knows in each, the facilitator invites them to look for relationships between the various spaces. As the explorer considers those relationships, not just conceptually but also spatially, the chance of a creative moment occurring increases exponentially. An explorer may suddenly realise that the whole network looks like a path or a spider's web. Seeing something through a new lens or a different metaphor like this may well unlock a creative solution to a long-standing problem or prompt an insight into an important goal.

This book is about how to facilitate the Clean Space process. You'll learn how to invite the explorer to locate spaces, to individuate each space and to relate them to one another. You'll learn about *psychoactivity* and *network effects* – signs that spontaneous creativity is in the air. And you'll discover how to bring the process to a conclusion and invite the explorer to articulate what they have learned.

And once you are competent at facilitating the *essential routines*, we'll introduce ideas for getting creative with the process itself and for adapting its use with groups.

As well as facilitating the explorer to put experiences in space, move around, relate spaces and connect up the network, there is an extra ingredient that makes Clean Space so effective. And that is the particular kind of facilitation you'll be engaged in: *clean* facilitation. This means using specific questions and directions to support the explorer to navigate their network of spaces. It means minimising your interventions, keeping your thoughts about what is happening to yourself and letting go of any desire you may have to fix a problem, suggest a solution or stimulate their creativity. It means noticing what is happening to the emergent network, paying close attention to the effects on the explorer and inviting them to attend to what is significant for them. In this way serendipitous moments, creative insights and solutions to old problems are given the opportunity to emerge.

While the immediate effects are nice to have, it is the longer-lasting benefits of working in this way that make all the difference. We have met people years later who are still enjoying the rewards of their Clean Space sessions; people who have:

○ Changed career

○ Created a better work-life balance

○ Improved relationships

○ Let go of limiting beliefs

○ Generated innovative ideas

○ Connected with what is most important to them

○ Accessed spiritual states

We created the short Clean Space activity at the start of this book to enable you to experience the process for yourself before you facilitate others.

We have given this mini-version to people who were learning how to be facilitators. Most of them had never tried Clean Space before and had no idea what to expect.

We've also used the mini-version to facilitate groups with each individual considering their own topic. Some of the comments people made afterwards are shown opposite. This very short version of Clean Space clearly had a sizeable impact. Our training rooms were buzzing!

"I spent ages trying to find the location of 'my thing'. I thought I'd found it and nothing came. So I moved and then information came. The first space was about the subject matter of the project. The second space was about the emotions of the project, and the third about why I am doing it."

"Moving between the first space and the second space was extraordinarily powerful — more powerful than I could have imagined. For me, it was the difference between positive and negative thoughts, heart and head, potentially success and failure. I changed my height, which I think was particularly powerful as it changed my body, which in turn changed my feelings."

"I wrote what I wanted and placed it. Then I came back to my chair to reflect and realised I was thinking about being on a balcony with the topic behind me. So I went out on the balcony and had it behind me and it was lovely — a fresh open horizon ahead of me, full of potential. The process was very revealing."

"I immediately saw my 'thing' from a different perspective and the distance between me and it was helpful."

"I didn't want to go back to the topic. In fact I turned around from it and it became more possible."

"It's blown me away a little bit. When I moved... the change, the physicality of standing there, sitting here... it was a completely multi-faceted view of my topic."

"It's such a weird sensation putting the piece of paper down, or positioning myself, and instinctively knowing if it is right or wrong. This is something that needs to be experienced to understand it."

HOW TO USE THIS BOOK

Clean Space is not a linear process; it is 3D, systemic, networked and emergent. The spaces the explorer identifies can be at any height and at any angle. But a book must proceed in a linear fashion from the front cover to the back.

Fortunately, you can choose to read it in any order; you can follow the order we've chosen or browse these short chapter descriptions and jump to whatever interests you.

If you're keen to start using the process straight away, the place to jump to is Chapter 2, where you'll find a basic Clean Space script.

If you learn best through examples, you'll find 16 case studies scattered throughout the book which illustrate various aspects of the process.

And if you are experienced with Clean Space you might be keen to see how the process can be used in other ways (Chapter 6) or with groups (Chapter 7).

Chapter 1 ...

... sets out the **conditions for creativity** that are intrinsic to Clean Space. Learn how context, location, individuation, relating, movement, iteration, integration, metaphor and clean all play their part in encouraging the new and the creative to unfold.

JUMP HERE FOR BASIC SCRIPT

Chapter 2 ...

... expands on the **clean** and **spatial** aspects of the process. You'll also find the **essential Clean Space questions and directions**, including a **script** (pages 60–61) you can follow as you learn the process.

Chapter 3 ...

... presents **guidelines for making choices** when certain conditions arise within a Clean Space session. **How you facilitate** is a vital part of creating a clean context for the explorer and this chapter outlines the basics.

Chapter 4 ...

... focuses on the conditions that can arise during Clean Space that indicate creative possibilities are afoot. We explain **emergence, psychoactivity, network effects and synchronicity** – and how to develop your capacity to attend to these phenomena.

Chapter 5 ...

... presents the **conditional questions and directions** These provide the flexibility you will need to navigate an explorer's unique journey to their creative outcomes.

Chapter 7 ...

... takes these ideas a step further and examines how to **use Clean Space with groups.** How is it like working with an individual? How is it different?

Chapter 6 ...

... is all about **how to get creative with the process itself.** How can you use it in different ways, combine it with other processes, deal with restrictions, limited space or limited mobility and design your own creativity processes?

Chapter 8 ...

... concludes the book with a **short review** of what we've covered along with an 'inner' Clean Space process you can use to **reflect on what you've learned**.

As you'll discover, Clean Space is iterative – it builds on itself – and you can expect learning Clean Space to be iterative as well. We revisit certain key ideas time and again each from a different angle. We also envisage you doing some reading, having a go, reading some more and deepening your learning each time. After a while, you'll have less need of the book, but it can still be useful to come back to it and discover even more depth in its pages.

Clean Space can be run as a step-by-step technique and in 30-40 minutes almost all explorers will get valuable results. And it can be so much more. We have written this book so those who wish to can go beyond the technology and embrace the original Greek meaning of 'technique' – the method used by an artist. An artist may employ standard techniques but if they are to produce something original, these cannot be applied formulaically.

Whatever your situation, whatever your learning style and whatever your needs, we hope that through this book you'll become a fan of Clean Space and the world of creative ideas it evokes.

In the end, creativity isn't just the things we choose to put in, it's the things we choose to leave out.

AUSTIN KLEON

Chapter 1

Conditions for Creativity

Conditions For Creativity

Problem-solving, innovation, management, leadership, conflict resolution, writing books, parenting… these and almost everything else in today's complex world require at least an element of creativity.

Creativity is all around us, in abundance. It is a natural process. Evolution itself is a creative process with life forms appearing one from another through the millennia, creating millions of species. Every single human being is a creation; each of us is unique with massive potential to think new thoughts, conjure up new ideas and create new things. With the invention of the internet, the number of ways we can express our creativity has increased exponentially; anyone can design a greetings card, publish a book, or buy the materials they need for virtually any creative project.

And yet many problems go unsolved, many companies lack the innovations they need to be successful, and many people undervalue their own creativity. Rather than seeing an abundance of creativity, we often bemoan its lack. We want more creativity – in our boardrooms, in our classrooms, in our lives.

So what makes creativity more likely to occur? Through our reading and experience we have identified a number of conditions:

- ➤ **Context:** including serendipity
- ➤ **Utilising space:** location matters
- ➤ **Individuating:** making distinctions
- ➤ **Relating:** making connections
- ➤ **Moving:** in physical and mental space
- ➤ **Iterating:** building or honing ideas
- ➤ **Integrating:** seeing the big picture
- ➤ **Metaphor:** juxtaposing ideas

What if there were a simple process that made use of all these conditions? And what if you could use it to facilitate someone else's, your own or a group's creativity?

Clean Space can do all this and more. But before we show you how it works, we are going to take you on a brief tour of why each of these conditions for creativity has a key part to play. Later you'll learn how Clean Space utilises these conditions, and how you can adapt them when you get creative with the process.

> Note, we use two types of bullet point:
> ◯ Denotes a list.
> ➤ Signposts sections that follow.

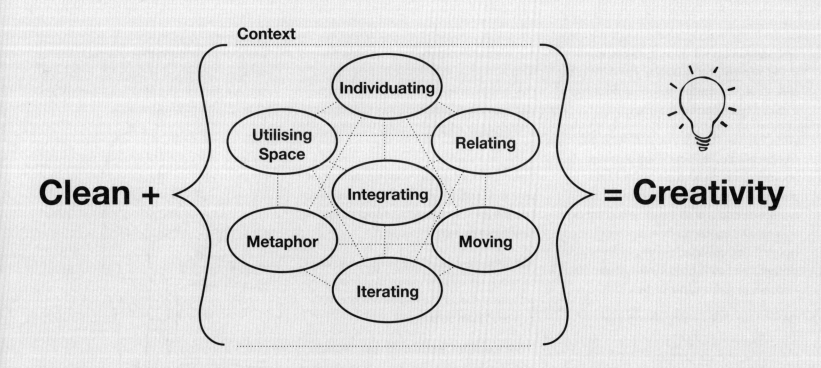

Clean + { Context

Individuating

Utilising Space

Relating

Integrating

Metaphor

Moving

Iterating

} **= Creativity**

Context: Including Serendipity

While a flash of inspiration takes place in a single moment, it is unlikely to come out of the blue. Creativity doesn't happen in isolation; it always takes place in a context.

When Einstein imagined himself riding on a beam of light, he already had questions about relativity on his mind. Viktor Frankl probably wouldn't have written one of the top-selling books of all time if he had not been incarcerated in Auschwitz. And James Dyson wouldn't have invented the bag-less vacuum cleaner if he hadn't been frustrated with his Hoover's diminishing performance.

Context is a vital yet slippery ingredient of creativity because it can include, among other things, the physical environment, the culture and our hopes, needs and desires.

It also includes chance events. Being open to what is happening in the world around us and how it might relate to a problem or what we want to achieve means we can spot potential solutions that might not otherwise have occurred to us.

Velcro came about when George de Mestral went for a walk in the country and wondered how the burrs attached to his socks could be turned into something useful.

And the current use of Viagra occurred when someone realised the marketing possibilities in the side effects of a heart medication that increased male potency.

These examples, and in fact most creative breakthroughs – whether they came about through a deliberate process or an unexpected surprise – have involved serendipity.

Serendipity is noticing the potential in chance events and utilising that potential. In this way, ideas are turned into outcomes – even when this is not what we had in mind.

George de Mestral investigates a burr under his microscope.

Utilising Space: Location Matters

Archimedes was in the bath.

In his study of ninety-one exceptionally creative individuals, Mihaly Csikszentmihalyi found that location was often more important to the creative process than we might imagine.

It matters that Archimedes was in the bath; he could not have had his eureka moment anywhere else. It may apocryphal but it is no coincidence that Sir Isaac Newton came up with the Theory of Gravity while sitting under an apple tree rather than a chaise longue. And while it's not immediately obvious why sitting on a train would lead J.K. Rowling to invent Harry Potter, it turns out the train was delayed which gave her four hours of uninterrupted thinking time.

In *The Big Small*, Steve Martin, Noah Goldstein and Robert Cialdini cite recent research studies which suggest that even the height of a ceiling, the way seats are arranged in a room, or small changes to the physical distance from which information is viewed can make a big difference to peoples' thinking.

Not only do these factors influence creativity, they determine the kind of creativity we can access:

○ High ceilings unconsciously prompt us to think generally and conceptually while low ceilings are likely to encourage specific, constrained thoughts.

○ A group that sits in a circle will typically focus on the group's collective objectives, while people in angular or square seating arrangements tend to be more self-orientated.

○ Solving a task can seem easier when you lean away or take a physical step back from the information.

Added to this, things look different when we move to a new place, whether that is the other side of the world or the other side of the street. When we turn round and look back at where we have just come from, the world often looks surprisingly different. *Where* we are matters.

Sir Isaac Newton was under an apple tree.

J.K. Rowling was on a train.

Individuating: Making Distinctions

Unattributed drawing, 1892, made famous by Ludwig Wittgenstein

According to the biblical story, creation started when God separated light from darkness and called the light 'Day' and the darkness 'Night'. God was making distinctions and naming things – individuating them.

By singling something out and differentiating it from other things we give it an identity and an existence separate from everything else. And naming something draws a boundary between what that thing is and what it is not.

It is said that when Walt Disney had an idea for a film he moved it around three rooms, each having a different function and offering a different perspective: the Dreamer, the Realist and the Critic. By separating these three functions he was able to distinguish which role he was in at any one time.

Marie Curie's work on radioactivity (a term she coined) gained her a Nobel Prize for physics. After spending years working in a converted shed to test her hunch that uranium ore contained new elements, she isolated polonium and radium and became the first person to be awarded a second Nobel laureate, this time for chemistry.

Individuating things changes the way we understand the world. Look at the picture on this page. Do you see a duck or a rabbit? To see either you need to distinguish some part of it, the beak or ears maybe. Then the whole of the duck or rabbit's head appears. By focusing on different features it is possible to switch between seeing either animal. But your brain will not allow you to see both at once. Your eyes see the same image but the distinctions you make change the picture.

Without distinctions there are no things, no ideas – nothing. And it is not until something is individuated that we can name it and start relating it to other things.

Relating:
Making Connections

Creativity relies on making connections by relating previously unrelated ideas. In a talk on *The Neuroscience of Creativity*, Baroness Susan Greenfield says creativity happens when the brain creates "unusual associations" and for the first time *here* is connected to *there* which means *this* is connected to *that*.

Post-it Notes came about through a chance connection between two 3M scientists – one who'd inadvertently invented a new glue which had no known application, and one who was looking for a way to mark his hymn book.

Relationships are rather mysterious things; not just relationships between people, but any relationship. As soon as two things, people or concepts are connected in some way there is a relationship between them. Since two things cannot occupy the same space at the same time, almost all relationships have a spatial element. Other relationships don't exist in the everyday physical world – you can't

see or hear or touch them – yet without them creativity would not exist.

Richard Ogle reports that when James Watson, Francis Crick and Rosalind Franklin were working to uncover the structure of DNA they found that:

> Once key ideas ... were connected, they began, quasi-autonomously, to make new sense in terms of one another, leading to the emergence of a whole that was more than the sum of its parts.

Whether we think in words, pictures, sounds or feelings, our brains are associative organs. One thing reminds us of something else, and before you know it we have related two things and a new idea pops up. Devising new solutions to old problems, giving birth to new ideas, or bringing an innovation to market all involve changing the way we perceive and connect existing relationships.

Creativity is just connecting things.
STEVE JOBS

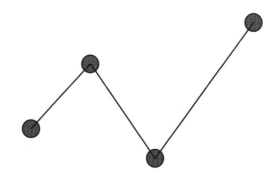

Moving:
In Physical and Mental Space

*All truly great thoughts
are conceived while
walking.*

FRIEDRICH NIETSCHE

Isadora Duncan famously said, "If I could say it, I wouldn't have to dance it."

Since at least the time of peripatetic Greek philosophers, there has been a deep, intuitive connection between moving and creativity. And it is not just dance. Beethoven, Tchaikovsky and Emmanuel Kant had daily walking rituals. Steve Jobs was known for his walking meetings.

Stanford University researchers Marily Oppezzo and Daniel Schwartz have found that walking boosts creative inspiration. They examined creativity levels of people while they walked versus while they were sitting. A person's creative output increased by an average of 60 percent when walking.

Travel broadens the mind. But so can moving from one side of a room to the other. The activity in the Preface will likely have demonstrated in a very real way how the simple act of moving from one space to another is much less predictable and can have a much greater effect than we might expect.

And it is not just the physical act of moving that can have a creative effect. Moving around in our own mind is one of our most creative abilities. We often take for granted the mental gymnastics required to enact these metaphors:

○ Stand in someone else's shoes

○ Step back and see the whole picture

○ Take a bird's eye view

○ Go beyond the obvious.

This ability means we can take 'leaps of thought' that are 'bounded' only by our imagination.

Iterating: Building or Honing Ideas

New ideas come from ideas that already exist – they build on one another.

During the 1820s Charles Babbage and Ada Lovelace created a 'computer' – a six-wheeled machine that could perform mathematical calculations. Their next version was just a bit different from their first and their next a bit different again. This iterative process has ultimately resulted in the iPhone.

Iteration can go in two directions; it either builds or it hones. Compound interest is a good example of how iterating can build: each year the interest is calculated by applying a simple formula which includes the previous year's interest.

The creative craft of improvisation also relies on the principle of iteration – building on ideas rather than money. And it also depends on the players following rules. One such rule is known as, 'Yes, and ...'. A player has to accept another's suggestion and then add a further idea. While this simple rule constrains players' behaviour, it also opens up possibilities and helps to ensure the audience stays around for the next scene.

Alternatively, we might start out with a number of options and through a process of elimination, iteratively and progressively work our way towards the best solution.

As Brendon Buchard points out:

Every artist, inventor, designer, writer, or other creative will talk about his work being an iterative experience. He'll start with one idea, shape it, move it, combine it, break it, begin anew, discover something within himself, see a new vision, go at it again, test it, share it, fix it, break it, hone it, hone it, hone it, hone it ... Willingness to iterate is what makes the world's most creative people so creative.

The more constraints one imposes, the more one frees one's self.

IGOR STRAVINSKY

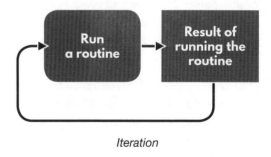

Iteration

Integrating: Seeing the Big Picture

Ideas have little value until they are organised, perhaps in our mind or with pen and paper. To do this we place the individual items somewhere. Think graphs, tables, charts, mind maps and decision trees. Each item on a graph or map has its own place and the connections between the items are signified by angles, distances and other relationships. This allows us to see the bigger picture, to notice patterns and to make sense of the constituent parts.

When a network of ideas gets complex enough we search for the simplicity of a higher-level integration. This brings with it knowledge and understanding which are not available from any of the parts on their own, for example:

○ In the 1880s, Williamina Fleming studied thousands of photographs of galaxies. After several years she noticed patterns that led to a brand new classification of stars based on their temperature.

○ Amazon aggregates data which enables them to suggest books you might like, based on your own preferences and those of others who buy similar books.

○ A group of scientists conducts a meta-analysis of many research studies which provides new information not available in any of the original pieces of research.

Combining, joining, merging, uniting, mixing or blending ideas until they become a whole are all ways to integrate. This can happen in a blinding flash, and it can occur so slowly we are unaware it is happening until the integration is complete. Integration occurs in many guises:

○ Summarising

○ Concluding

○ Insight

○ Pattern detection

○ Metaphor

○ Categorising

○ Intuition

○ Learning

○ Habit

Even our sense of the space around us relies on an integration of visual, auditory, tactile and proprioceptive information, since humans do not have any way of sensing space directly.

Integration brings things together and provides the glue that keeps them together. It is fundamental to the creative process. Each of Walt Disney's Dreamer, Realist and Critic perspectives is valuable on its own, and together they produced some of the best-loved cartoons of all time.

Metaphor: Juxtaposing Ideas

One feature of creativity has already appeared 'quietly' within all the other conditions – and that is metaphor.

Disney thought of himself as a "little bee going from one area of the studio to another, gathering pollen and stimulating everyone." Mozart was "constantly looking for two notes that loved each other." And writer Rita Mae Brown reckons "Creativity is a power, intensifying life."

Disney, Mozart and Brown are not the only people to use metaphor to think and talk about the creative process. It is almost impossible not to. Consider these well-known phrases:

- ○ Incubating ideas
- ○ Making a creative leap
- ○ Thinking outside the box
- ○ Blending ideas from different fields
- ○ Looking at things from different angles

These are all metaphors. Metaphor involves using something tangible as a way to understand, describe and reason about something complex or abstract. It can be both a source for and the result of creativity. Thinking metaphorically – being able to transfer ideas from one area to another – is itself a creative process. It has been the basis of many inventions and breakthroughs in science. As James Geary says in *I Is An Other*:

> A metaphor juxtaposes two different things and then skews our point of view so unexpected similarities emerge. Metaphorical thinking half discovers and half invents the likenesses it describes.

It was not until 1980 that George Lakoff and Mark Johnson's systematic analysis in *Metaphors We Live By* woke the world up to the notion that our everyday metaphors are indispensible to thought and are firmly rooted in our embodied physical experience. And it was 2011 before anyone thought to create an experiment to see whether we really are more creative when sitting outside a box than in it. We are, it seems.

We speak, on average, six metaphors a minute but we barely notice this. And we notice the metaphorical use of space – the most common source of metaphors in all languages – even less. The idea that we might take a person's metaphors as perfect descriptions of their inner experience was central to David Grove's work in the 1980s and 1990s – yet it is still a radical idea today.

So Where Does 'Clean' Fit In?

Clean Language is deeply agreeable to the client's heart and soul.

DAVID GROVE

All the conditions we've explored so far – utilising context, considering location and spatial arrangements, making distinctions and connections, moving around, building or honing existing ideas, seeing the big picture and thinking metaphorically – can prepare for and stimulate creative breaks in our habitual patterns.

While other processes use some of these conditions to stimulate creativity, Clean Space uses them all. It is also different because of its 'clean' way of working and its emphasis on utilising the metaphor of a physical network.

A clean approach is based on a number of assumptions:

○ Every person or group has the ability to generate new ideas and come up with creative solutions.

○ Facilitator content complicates and potentially undermines others' creativity.

○ Minimal intervention provides maximal opportunity for others' creativity to flourish.

○ Unless you use Clean Language you will *unintentionally* add your own ideas and metaphors into their mix.

○ Change happens *spontaneously* because individuals and groups are self-organising systems.

When a person or group is supported to generate a network of their ideas, they not only learn how to apply their creativity to a particular problem or desired outcome, they also strengthen their creative muscles.

Prior to Clean Space, David Grove had already developed a brilliant way of encouraging people to access their innate creativity – a methodology he called Clean Language.

Clean Language utilises the metaphors people use naturally as they speak. If one of his clients said, "It's like I have butterflies in my stomach," then rather than treat this as a figure of speech, he would ask questions such as:

○ And where in your stomach are those butterflies?

○ And what kind of butterflies are those butterflies?

○ And is there anything else about stomach with butterflies?

David called this way of working 'clean' because he used the client's exact words, taking them at face value and asking questions which did not 'contaminate' their experience with his metaphors, assumptions or interpretations.

Clean Space required an extension to the Clean Language set of questions and, for the first time, the addition of 'clean directions' – statements that invite the explorer to do something. As you will see, in Clean Space most directions request the explorer to move.

And where in your stomach are those butterflies?

Space is what stops everything from happening in the same place.

ARTHUR C. CLARKE

Chapter 2

Space to Think

Space to Think

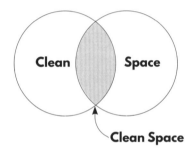

Clean **Space**

Clean Space

It all sprang from the intersection of two ideas.

In late 2001 David Grove travelled from the States to New Zealand as the only passenger on a container cargo ship. This gave him plenty of time – and space – to think. And while looking out across the vast space of the Pacific Ocean, he had a really good idea.

The physical and spatial nature of metaphor had always intrigued David. At one time he and his then wife Cei Davies Lynn ran a retreat centre which had a lake, a hill and a wood. If a client's key metaphors corresponded to any of these, David would go with them to the equivalent physical environment to continue the therapeutic work there. By externalising their internal symbolic world, a client could experience changes they would be unlikely to have any other way.

But on that ship he began to wonder if space could hold different kinds of information and what would happen if the clients physically moved around those spaces. What did

someone know when they were in a real corner? And how was that different from what they knew when they were by a window, or in a doorway, behind a chair or in the middle of an empty room? What else would they know when they were standing near to, or far from, something that represented what they wanted or their problem? We like to imagine him testing out these ideas – wandering around the ship and asking himself, *And what do I know here?* moving to a new spot and then asking, *And what do I know here?*

By the time he arrived in New Zealand, his focus of attention had shifted from metaphor and language to movement and networks of spaces. And it all sprang from the intersection of two almost mystical ideas:

○ A space can hold information.

○ The less a facilitator contributes the more a person will access their own creativity.

In other processes that utilise space, the names of the spaces and their physical locations are usually pre-determined and managed by the facilitator. In David's new process, the location of the spaces would be determined by his client who would give them any names they liked. Moreover, the spaces were not decided in advance; they would become apparent one at a time as the process unfolded. At all stages, neither the facilitator nor the client would know what was going to happen next. In one genius move David had created a new spatial process that was clean and emergent – and he called it Clean Space.

As David brought in ideas from network theory the process morphed and changed from week to week. After a few years, Clean Space evolved into a suite of processes called *Emergent Knowledge*.

James, together with Penny Tompkins, published their first model of Clean Space in 2003. Over time the number of variations grew and to some extent the core of the process started to get lost.

After David died in 2008 James and Penny revisited everything that by then came under the rubric of Clean Space. They produced a 'lite' or cut-down version that contained only the basic elements which could easily be learned by novice facilitators.

Writing this book has caused us (Marian and James) to revisit what is central and what is peripheral to the process. In deconstructing the model and working through the function of every question and every direction, we have sought to get closer to the essence of the process, to the defining operations and to the core principles.

Our model has a similar shape to the one David presented in the first Clean Space workshop in New Zealand – and it has some fundamental differences. For example, questions from previous Clean Language methods have been dropped, directions have been refined and the process has been simplified – but the principles of clean remain. David's original version was the 'seed' from which all the later versions developed, just like the Babbage and Lovelace computer was the forerunner of today's iPhone.

Before we unveil our new model, let's look in a bit more detail at what it means to be clean and about inner and outer space.

What Does it Mean to be Clean?

About how fast were the cars going?

It is easy to be influenced without realising it. As early as the 1970s research by Elizabeth Loftus and her colleagues found that the way in which questions were worded altered subjects' memories of events they had witnessed. Loftus showed that changing a single word in a question could make a difference. After watching a film of a car accident five groups were asked, "About how fast were the cars going when they X into each other?" Significantly different estimates were given depending whether 'X' was *smashed* (41mph), *collided* (39mph), *bumped* (38mph), *hit* (34mph) or *contacted* (32mph). In another experiment, being asked, "Did you see *the* broken headlight?" instead of, "Did you see *a* broken headlight?" doubled the chances of a subject being led to say they had seen a broken headlight when there were none in the film.

In the field of therapy the issue of influence is an important one. People are paying to be influenced and yet when they are at their most vulnerable they may be more open to unwanted, unproductive or unhelpful suggestions than usual. For many years it has been acknowledged that taking a client-centred approach is a good way for therapists to guard against leading their clients. But when David Grove observed well-known psychotherapists working, he noticed that however well they listened, the simple mechanics of conversation – reflecting, paraphrasing, summarising – made it virtually impossible for them to avoid changing their clients' language and substituting their own. This particularly applied to implicit metaphors that are processed below everyday levels of awareness.

For example, did you notice in the previous sentence that 'applied', 'implicit' 'process', 'below' and 'levels' are all metaphors? Any attempt to paraphrase or rewrite the sentence will involve introducing different metaphors. This doesn't matter so much in ordinary conversation but it does matter when what is being changed is an expression of a person's inner experience. This kind of subtle 'imposition' can 'contaminate' the original experience, 'making it harder' for them to know their own mind.

David's solution to this problem was to minimise the use of metaphors and assumptions in his questions and to limit himself to using only words spoken by the client. He honed his questions over many years until they were as minimal and as neutral as they could be. He wanted the "I-ness of the therapist to appear to cease to exist".

When people who spend a lot of time listening to others first come across the notion of 'clean' they often remark that this is what they do anyway. And they may – but not consistently. It means more than asking a few clean questions. It's about your whole approach to a person and their inner world.

Instead of someone who adds in ideas and solutions in the hope that some will be useful, being a clean facilitator means keeping out of the way and setting up the conditions so a person's natural creativity emerges organically, all by itself. When outside concepts, suggestions, reframes, helpful hints and so on are excluded, what does the explorer have left? They have no option but to fall back on their own resources and reflections and to use these in novel and creative ways.

We create an environment in which the client can discover where it is that he needs to go... information evolves internally out of the client's experience. It is not introduced into the client's experience by the therapist.

DAVID GROVE & BASIL PANZER

Inner and Outer Space

Space plays a role in all our behaviour. We live in it, move through it, explore it, defend it.

JOHN O'KEEFE

Space is a common feature of our world. So common in fact, that much of the time we take it for granted.

The moment we enter a space, we instantly size it up, consciously or unconsciously. When you go into a cinema or theatre, how do you decide where to sit? Do you prefer to be near the front or the back? On the left or right? On the edge or in the middle? Whether we know it or like it, our bodies are constantly reacting to the configuration of our surroundings.

Space is also inherent in our inner, private, world – what cognitive scientists call our *mental space*. Having studied hundreds of people, social scientist Lucas Derks has coined the term Social Panorama to describe how, when we think of people we know, we unconsciously put images of those people in particular mental places.

There is nothing random about this; according to Derks, *relationship equals location*. If someone is 'close' to us metaphorically speaking, they will be nearby in our Social Panorama. If we 'look up' to someone, chances are we'll see them above us in our mental space. If they 'stand beside' us or we 'follow in their footsteps', they'll be in a corresponding position in our imagination.

As a way to test this he suggests thinking about someone you love. Where are they in your mind's eye? What about someone you don't know very well, like a shop assistant? What happens if you swap their positions for a moment? According to Derks, most people who try this swap experience "a strong resistance as if the first position is only reserved for a very special person".

The ability to use space to represent relationship metaphorically is not confined to the way we think about people. It also applies to things, abstract concepts and emotions... in fact to almost everything. The 'bottom line' is that we are hard 'pushed' to describe any 'inner' experience without 'turning to' metaphors that involve spatial relationships. Location, distance, height, angle, etc. are all in relation to something or someone. And they are important because we cannot help but give them meaning.

If that isn't strange enough, we also reverse the process. We organise the exterior world (mostly unconsciously) so that it corresponds to the configuration of our interior metaphor map. For example, while writing this book, we laid out some sections on the floor, and Marian 'had to' swap two of them around because they did not feel right to her. She felt at ease when the tension created by the incongruence between inner and outer worlds was resolved.

While people like artists, architects, town planners and designers make a living from utilising the interplay between inner and outer space, we are all engaged in these kinds of creative acts. Whether we're choosing places to visit, where to live, the kind of home to live in, organising furniture and ornaments, arranging food on a plate, or even how we hang out the washing, we're involved in a creative interchange between inner and outer spatial relations.

Space is so fundamental to perception that Steven Pinker contends the metaphor of space acts like the "medium of thought itself". He draws this conclusion because:

Location in space is one of the two fundamental metaphors in language, used for thousands of meanings. ... Many cognitive scientists (including me) have concluded from their research on language that a handful of concepts about places, paths, motions ... underlie the literal or figurative meanings of tens of thousands of words and constructions, not only in English but in every other language that has been studied.

Clean Space makes the 'medium of thought itself' visible, malleable and in service to the creative process.

Clean Space: A Context for Creativity

Clean Space fosters creativity through establishing a network of spaces – and establishing that network is in itself a creative process. It is a way of working that constrains the facilitator's language and behaviour so that they say and do less. As a result the explorer puts more attention on the way their inner world works, which paves the way for their system to learn from itself.

When you facilitate someone with Clean Space, your job is two-fold: to give minimal direction – just enough to keep the process going; and to calibrate what's happening for the explorer. It's an exercise in restraint. The facilitator needs to be alert to naturally occurring conditions for creativity, go with them, and when appropriate, invite the explorer to become aware of them too.

The process starts with the facilitator having paper or Post-it Notes and pens available and inviting the explorer to:

Write or draw your desired outcome or topic of interest.

Whatever they put on the paper becomes the context and a starting point. It sets the direction for the whole session. Every word or mark on the paper can make a difference.

Think back to the Preface and your own exploration. Would an extra word or one word fewer have made a difference? What if you had framed a problem as a desired outcome – or a desired outcome as a problem? Drawn a picture instead of writing or vice versa?

The importance of the topic rests with the explorer. As a facilitator you will often have minimal interest in it; you may not even know what it is. Some people fold their paper over, turn it upside down or just draw a squiggle, while others write a clear statement and read it out loud. Some people offer an explanation; others do not. It doesn't matter. As we'll explain later, your job, throughout the process, will be to pay attention to:

○ How the explorer is using the space

○ The spatial metaphors they use

○ The configuration of spaces

○ Movement of the explorer's body

○ Potentially serendipitous moments

○ The way the explorer reacts to what they're discovering.

Any or all of these may be an opening into a rich seam of creativity.

Having set the context, the next thing to do is to establish a network of spaces in relation to the topic. Clean Space is based on the premise that physical space can have psychological and symbolic meaning. David Grove recognised that when a person creates a network of meaningful spaces a new context emerges. This enables the explorer to not only examine their own thoughts and feelings in new ways, but to also generate new experiences, right there and then.

Then fascinating and unexpected things happen. Explorers get new perspectives on old problems, have flashes of inspiration, experience deep insights into the nature of their situation, feel changes happening, make decisions, come to conclusions, plan their next steps. Since everything that happens in Clean Space emanates from the explorer, they know the results are down to them.

As a Clean Space facilitator, you will need to trust that staying clean will indeed result in creative insights and solutions for the explorer. You'll need to let go of any desire you have to chip in and be helpful or to have more than a rudimentary understanding of what's going on. You'll also need to trust that the explorer really can sort out their own thinking, solve their own problems and access their own innate creativity.

Establishing a Network of Spaces

A *network* consists of a number of items, known as *nodes*, interconnected by a number of *links*, which together form a system.

Clean Space facilitates a person to build a network of experiences one space at a time. The explorer establishes a spatial network by going through four essential routines:

- ➤ Start
- ➤ Establish Spaces
- ➤ Establish Links
- ➤ Finish

We call these routines 'essential' since without them there will not be a network and without a network there can be no Clean Space process.

Throughout these routines the explorer continually responds, consciously or unconsciously, to what is happening to their network. When features of the network emerge spontaneously we call them *network effects*.

Attending to these effects is how Clean Space becomes a personalised process.

Network effects are *emergent properties* – the characteristics and functions of a network that appear spontaneously at a certain level of complexity. They cannot be predicted by examining any of the individual spaces or even from the relationships between them. They result from the pattern of those relationships.

The difference between a formulaic technique and Clean Space relates to how the facilitator responds when an explorer does something 'out of the ordinary'. Commonly, this is seen as a problem and what happens is either ignored or made to fit the technique. In Clean Space, however, the unexpected is not a problem – it's the process working; it is the purpose of all the establishing, moving, relating, iterating etc.

By acknowledging and working with the surprising and unexpected events that occur, the process changes from a general format into something personalised for the individual. Noticing network effects and, under certain conditions, directing the explorer to attend to them is the artistry of facilitating Clean Space.

We have included network effects in the following diagrams for completeness and to indicate their importance. But it won't be until Chapter 4 that we'll explain in detail how to recognise and utilise network effects.

For now we will summarise what happens in each of the essential routines and show you how they make use of just six clean questions and six clean directions.

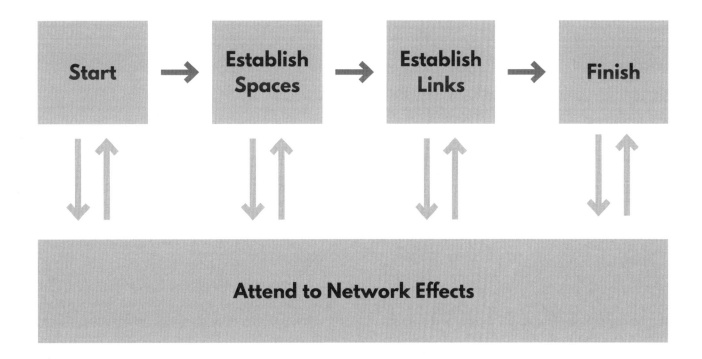

Start

Building a network from scratch means first establishing the initial nodes of that network. The Start routine establishes the first two nodes: a space for the explorer's chosen topic and an initial location for the explorer (Space 1). This automatically creates a spatial relationship between the topic and the explorer, providing the grain of sand from which the pearl of the network will grow.

It also establishes a place to come back to, and acts as a 'reference point' against which the effects of the process can be compared at the end.

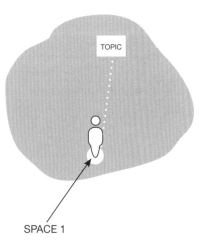

SPACE 1

Establish Spaces

This routine encourages the explorer to establish several new spaces, each node adding complexity and richness to the network. As the explorer locates, knows and marks each new space, those spaces – and the knowledge they hold – become individuated. Once the number of spaces gets to four or five most explorers have to give up trying to remember everything said or working out what will happen next. They become curious participants who contribute to rather than control what is happening to their network.

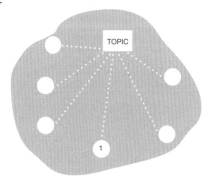

Attend to Network Effects

While spaces and links are being established the explorer will be responding to what is happening. Many of their responses will be internal and you will never know about them. Others will be visible or audible and some will be more significant than others. Occasionally the explorer's responses will demand a reaction from you, for example, if they can't physically get to a space they want to go to. Network effects are indicators that the space has become psychoactive: the configuration of the network is producing emergent properties, which the explorer's mind-body is reacting to.

Establish Links

Establishing links involves the explorer returning to a space, updating what is known there and then discovering the relationships between that space and the other spaces. Establishing links keeps the whole network alive and gives the explorer a sense of how it all fits together. It is also a way for the explorer to update their knowing in each space as the iterations take effect. As small changes cascade around the network their effects are amplified and consolidated creating a contagion of further unexpected happenings and discoveries. This routine also serves to check the ecology of the network from multiple perspectives – to ensure all the spaces are involved and have their say.

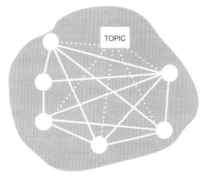

Finish

When it seems the explorer has extracted enough from the process, they are returned, as David Grove would say, "from whence they came" – to the original Space 1. This routine encourages the explorer to reflect on what has happened, the effects of that, and the effect of those effects. The explorer can consider how they now relate to the topic, compared to how they related to it at the start of the activity. It's a reality check: have they just been wandering around a room or has something happened to change the way they perceive or feel about their topic? This is also a practical way for the explorer to fully return to the physical world.

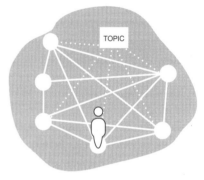

Attend to Network Effects

You may decide that some network effects are significant enough that you will invite the explorer to attend to them. To do so you will need to make use of one or more conditional questions or directions before returning to whichever essential routine you had been facilitating before. We focus on network effects in Chapters 4 and 5.

Getting Started

When you are ready to try your hand at facilitating someone using Clean Space, we recommend you start by learning to use *only* the essential routines: Start, Establish Spaces, Establish Links, Finish.

Each of the essential routines comprises a number of *invitations*, listed opposite. Each invitation involves at least one clean *direction* or clean *question*.

All the invitations, apart from the first and last, fit into six categories:

Directions:

- ○ Locate space
- ○ Mark space
- ○ Return to space

Questions:

- ○ Know here
- ○ Know about there
- ○ Update knowing

We recommend you use the questions an[d] directions *exactly* as printed and in the [order] recommended in the guidelines in the [next] chapter.

All invitations are in the present tens[e ...] apart from the first and last, they a[ll start with] the connecting word, 'And …'. Dis[tinguishing] between questions and directions [is important.] For the moment, just be aware that directions are specific instructions which invite the explorer to do something, in most cases to move location.

Not long after he had seen David Grove's first forays into Clean Space, James was invited to give a two-hour workshop at NASA's Goddard Space Flight Center. He thought it would be interesting for 30 engineers and scientists familiar with exploring outer space to explore inner space. After a brief introduction he handed everyone a piece of paper and asked them to write or draw an existing work

[...] wanted some [...] monstrated with [...] ut step-by-step [...] hat follow. In pairs [...] ach to facilitate [...] ucted to only do [...] ndout.

[...] ed that complete novices [...] results in just 20 minutes having [...] essential routines.

To get started, you will need an explorer who is willing to have a go, plus:

- ○ A space to work in – anything from a small room or hallway to a whole house or community hall, or an outdoor space such as a garden or park
- ○ A sheet of blank paper
- ○ Pen(s) or pencil(s)
- ○ Some Post-it Notes
- ○ The Step-by-Step Guide on pages 60-61.

Summary of Essential Questions and Directions

Start	Establish Spaces	Establish Links	Finish
Choose topic • Write or draw your desired outcome or topic of interest.			
Locate space • And place that where it needs to be. • And place yourself where you are now in relation to that. *[that = topic]*	**Locate space** • And find another space.	**Return to space** • And return to one of the other spaces.	**Return to space** • And return to *[Space 1]*.
Know here • And what do you know here?	**Know here** • And what do you know here?	**Update knowing** • And now what do you know here?	**Update knowing** • And knowing all that *[gesture around the network]* what do you know here now?
Know about there • And is there anything else you know here about that *[topic]*?	**Know about there** • And is there anything else you know here about that *[topic]*?	**Know about there** • And is there anything else you know here about *[other space]*?	
Mark Space • And what could this space be called? • And write the name of this space and use the Post-it to mark this space. *(This is Space 1.)*	**Mark Space** • And what could this space be called? • And mark this space *[with Post-it Note]*.		
			Complete • And what difference does knowing that make? • When you are ready, collect up your paper and Post-it Notes.

A Step-by-Step Guide to Using the Essential Routines

Facilitator's directions and questions are in bold.

Start

Provide the explorer with paper and pen(s).

Write or draw your desired outcome or topic of interest.

When they have written or drawn the topic ...

And place that where it needs to be.

'That' is the paper, so gesture to the paper as you say the word 'that' and whenever the topic is referred to.

When they have placed the paper ...

And place yourself where you are now in relation to that.

When they have stopping moving, wherever they are is Space 1.

And what do you know here?

When the explorer has finished thinking and speaking...

And is there anything else you know here, about that?

And what could this space be called?

Hand the explorer a pen and a pad of Post-its.

And write the name of this space and use the Post-it to mark this space.

Establish Spaces

And find another space.

When they have found a space ...

And what do you know here?

And is there anything else you know here, about that?
[Gesture to 'that' and optionally add 'there'.]

And what could this space be called?

Hand the client a pen and a Post-it pad. *[If the explorer seems to want to hang onto their pen and Post-its, let them.]*

And mark this space.

Repeat this routine until six spaces have been established (including Space 1).

Establish Links

And return to one of the other spaces.

When they have returned to a space...

And now what do you know here?

And what do you know here about *[gesture to one of the other spaces and optionally use the name of the space]***?**

Continue to ask **And what do you know here about [...]?** for each of the other spaces in any order.

Repeat this routine until all the spaces have been revisited once or you run out of time.

Finish

And return to *[gesture to Space 1].*

When they have returned to Space 1...

And knowing all that *[gesture around the network]* **what do you know here now?**

And what difference does knowing that make?

When you are ready, collect up your paper and Post-it Notes.

Case study 1: That person

While there is no substitute for a direct experience of Clean Space, we have included plenty of case studies to help you understand the process and learn about the choices facilitators make in the moment.

When observing a Clean Space session or reading a transcript it is difficult to know what is happening for the explorer. Often there is little traditional content and from the outside it is hard to appreciate how much of an effect shifting to a new position can have on the explorer's inner world. So we start with a case study written from the explorer's perspective. What is it like to go through the process? What happens? What are the benefits? Does it really work?

This session was led by Marian and took place within a Clean Space workshop. Apart from a brief introduction, the explorer had no knowledge of Clean Space or any real idea of what could happen. Here is her account:

"I had a problem with my line manager: she was bullying me at work. At the start of my Clean Space session I wrote 'that person' on a piece of paper and placed it near the fireplace. All I wanted was to run away and hide, to pretend the problem wasn't happening. So I got under the table. I was feeling quite fearful. But while I was there I realised I couldn't hide away.

"So I came out and sat on the sofa. This felt like being at home, safe in my house. I was surprised that even moving from under the table to the sofa – a few yards away – helped me feel less anxious and even relaxed.

"I next stood in the corner of the room. This was the first time I was *standing* in a space – and I realised I was perceiving 'that person' as sitting down. This gave me a sense of power. I recalled situations from the past when I had been in powerful positions and I thought to myself, 'Yes, I can be powerful'."

"Sitting at the table reminded me of my study at home and was another nice, resourceful space. I like to study and to think things through – and as I sat there, I thought about how I could be sensible and do something to resolve the situation. In this space, I realised that this was an emotional problem and it was my emotions that needed to be resolved.

"Then I went to the window – and when I looked out at the panorama in front of me, I thought about how massive the world is in comparison to my problem in the room. I thought, 'It's as though I could go from here through a portal to other places.' I thought about other job options and started putting things into perspective.

"In another space, near to 'that person' by the fireplace, I thought about all the lovely people in the organisation I work for and that if I decided to leave the job, I'd be leaving them, too. I felt mixed emotions and confusion.

"As the session went on, I began using the spaces to experience thinking about my problem in different ways. I could go to 'study' if I wanted to think; I could sit on the sofa any time I wanted to relax and I could go back to the corner for a surge of power. I could feel my anxiety levels reducing.

"I had initially seen 'that person' as quite demonic. I thought she was attacking me personally, questioning my ability and wanting me to leave the organisation. But there was a point while I was in a 'shared space' when I suddenly felt closer to her. Her persona changed and I saw her as a human being. I realised I wanted to have a conversation with her. As that happened I knew we would be able to move on from this and it would be resolved. Getting close to her changed how I was seeing her – and that was a big transformation.

"Right at the end of the session I remember saying it was as though I had started with a problem as big as a beach ball. It had then become tennis-ball sized and by the end it was the size of a marble. It was as though it had literally been shrinking in front of me.

"After the session I wrote to 'that person' and then we had a conversation. I told her how I had been feeling and how I would have preferred her to behave – and as we spoke, I felt really heard. There is a new, conciliatory dynamic between us now. We've moved on more productively than I would have thought possible. We've re-established a good working relationship."

I had started with a problem as big as a beach ball. It had then become tennis-ball sized and by the end it was the size of a marble.

Case Study 2: Gaining a Global Awareness

We've just seen how Clean Space results in a process that's alive and buzzing for the explorer. What's it like from the facilitator's viewpoint?

We've chosen this particular case study because, for the most part, the facilitator (James) stays within the essential routines. And there is also a preview of the kinds of things that can happen that we are calling network effects and to see how James responds to them.

Start

This session starts in a living room, furnished with sofas. James begins by offering the explorer, Lewis, a piece of paper and a few coloured pens. He invites him to, *Write or draw your desired outcome or topic of interest.*

Lewis writes a few words on the paper, which James is unable to read. When James invites

Lewis to place the paper where it needs to be, he puts it on the back of a sofa, then moves it and turns it upside down before returning it to its original spot. James waits, and when Lewis seems content with the placement James continues, *And place yourself where you are now in relation to that,* gesturing to the topic as he says 'that'.

The explorer moves around the room and settles on the threshold between the living room and the kitchen, facing into the living room. "Here," he says.

And what do you know here?

"Half of me is moving into that area *[gestures in front]* and half of me is staying in how it is now *[gestures behind]*."

And is there anything else you know here about that *[gestures to topic]*?

"I know I'm not facing it *[the topic]* directly. It's in my peripheral vision and that surprises me."

James invites Lewis to name and mark the space. He calls it Half and Half. This is Space 1.

Establish Space 2

James invites Lewis, *And find another space.* Lewis steps into the living room, walks around and places himself at an angle to the topic.

And what do you know here?

"I don't seem to want to face it directly so I'm wondering how ready I am... how happy I am to make it happen. When I think about it, I am ready, and I'm noticing I have an aversion to facing it directly."

And is there anything else you know here about that?

"It would be nice – and I'm questioning how much I want it."

Lewis names this space Reality Check.

Establish Space 3

When he is invited to find another space, Lewis goes to a place in the kitchen. James moves so he can see into the kitchen.

And what do you know here?

"I can't even see what I've written, but there's plenty in here to take my attention. This place produces things I enjoy that please myself and others. I get a lot of kudos, appreciation and benefit from staying here. And that *[gesturing to topic]* remains just a nice-to-have."

And is there anything else you know here about that *[gestures to topic]***?**

"From here it feels a bit either/or. Either I'm in the kitchen doing things that come easy or out there creating that. Doing this would mean giving up that. And I'm finding things here to take my attention – like I didn't put the lid on the honey pot."

Lewis names this space Either / Or.

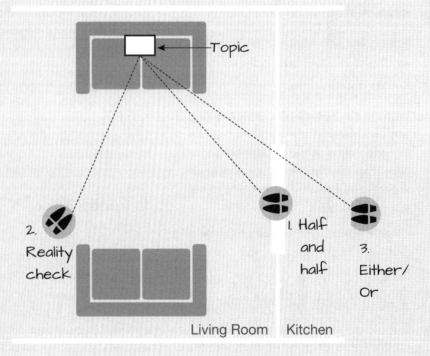

Establish Space 4

The explorer next returns to the living room and moves to a space facing the topic.

And what do you know here?

"Where I was in Reality Check *[Space 2]* was on a diagonal. The minute I stood here, I thought, 'This is perpendicular.' And somehow where I am standing now with my topic directly in front, the kitchen in my peripheral vision seems significant."

And is there anything else you know here about that *[gestures to topic]*?

"They negate each other, and allow neither. What I need is a different relationship with both of these."

And what could this space be called?

"This is a new formation. There's a line there *[indicates a line between the topic and Space 4]* and there's this line here *[indicates another line, perpendicular and immediately in front of him]*. I am connected to that from here. Actually what it is, is an 'I'. A capital I."

Lewis writes 'Capital I' on his Post-it and marks the space.

Establish Space 5

When James invites him to find another space, Lewis stays still for a long time before taking a tiny step backwards. Without waiting for a question, he says, "I don't know what's happening. That *[gestures towards the kitchen]* is in my peripheral vision. It's not taking my attention. Maybe this is the place I need to be. I don't want to move. I'm trying to. It was just a little step back. That is astounding!"

Since Lewis has indicated he is in a new space and has already started to describe his experience, the usual question, *And what do you know here?* seems redundant. So James keeps the process going by skipping that question and asking:

And is there anything else you know here about that *[gestures to topic]*?

"I get a sense of me doing it. A faint sense of it happening. I don't feel like I'm going to go and do it, but I have a sense of it happening over there *[gestures to topic]*."

And what could this space be called?

"Possibility," he says.

Establish Space 6

When invited to find another space, Lewis tries out a couple of places before settling in a spot behind another sofa. He stands there a while, before saying, "OK". He continues, "The interesting thing about this space is from here when the sun shines on my topic, it just looks like a blank piece of paper. I can't see anything on it. I feel like I've lost a bit of my connection with it. I realise my body is angled more towards the distraction in the kitchen. But what's stopping me heading there is that now I have an awareness of being outside of the Either/Or. This is a new place to be; it's more of a global awareness."

The explorer is now deep in thought, so James waits until Lewis comes out of his reverie. James skips two questions, going straight on to:

And what could this space be called?

"Global Awareness," Lewis replies.

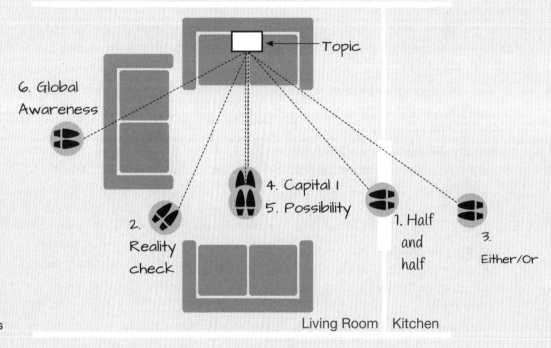

While James has been facilitating Lewis to establish six spaces, all kinds of interesting things have been happening which fall into the category of network effects:

- ○ **Body engaging with the space:** *[lots of gesturing]* ... just a little step back ... my body is angled

- ○ **Spatial metaphors:** half of me is moving, half is staying ... I'm not facing it directly ... on a diagonal ... perpendicular ... line ... connected ... lost my connection ... outside

- ○ **Spontaneous reactions:** that surprises me ... I'm noticing I have an aversion ... the minute I stood here, I thought ... that is astounding

James has chosen not to put additional attention on any of these, partly in the interests of getting the network established, partly because he is following the principle of making minimal interventions, and partly because there have been so many network effects, it would have been difficult for him to decide that any one was more significant than the others.

Now however, Lewis's comment, "This is a new place to be; it's more of a global awareness" suggests his attention is on the whole network – and this is significant enough for James to invite him to establish links with Global Awareness immediately rather than inviting him to return to another space.

Establish Links with Space 6 (Global Awareness)

And is there anything else you know here about *[gesture to Reality Check]***?**

"I realise what's happening here is another form of reality check. That space there is a more specific reality check, but here I have more of a sense how I am using my own thinking and attention to not pay attention to that *[gestures to topic]*. This is not an isolated incident – it's more general."

And is there anything else you know here about Capital I**?**

"Something was happening over there. It was an important place for me to stay and find out more. From here, outside of the whole thing, I'm trying to think about Capital I and there's still something about it... *[pause]* ... that I'm not sure of."

And is there anything else you know here about Possibility?

"Those two *[indicating Possibility and Capital I]* are related. I can't fool myself in either of those two places. I couldn't move forward, so I just took that small step back. That's a not-fooling-myself, joint space."

And is there anything else you know here about *[gestures to Either/Or]*?

"I like Either/Or a lot. I like being there. It's familiar, more comfortable, easier and fun – and I get all kinds of strokes. But now it feels as though when I'm giving in to easy and fun, I'm giving up the opportunity to create my topic. My topic means sitting with the unfamiliar, and it might become a struggle and uncomfortable. But with the awareness I have here I can see it's creative – that's the nature of creativity."

And is there anything else you know here about *[gestures to Half and Half]*?

"Half and Half would be easy if the pull of what's familiar and easy would just go away, but it's not going away. So it may be about combining both halves? Not giving up the familiar and fun half, but having the creativity half come with it somehow."

When James invites Lewis...

And return to one of the other spaces.

... he goes to Space 2, Reality Check.

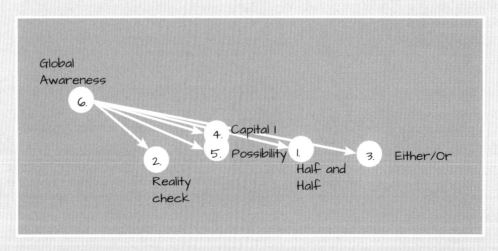

Establish Links with Space 2 (Reality Check)

And now, what do you know here?

"It was really useful to have seen this from a more global perspective. I can see all the spaces from here and I want to go back to the Capital I and Possibility there. That's where I want to be; that's where I need to be. At the end of the day, an action or decision is going to need to be taken and it's not going to happen from here."

And is there anything else you know here about *[gesture to Half and Half]***?**

"Nothing really."

And is there anything else you know here about *[gesture to Either/Or]***?**

"Over there in the kitchen I saw the lid had been left off the honey, and here I see how that takes my attention away from my topic."

Since the explorer has already referenced Capital I, Possibility and Global Awareness from here, James does not establish further links with them. Instead, he continues with ...

And return to one of the other spaces.

Although the explorer says he wants to be at Capital I and Possibility, he goes to Either/Or.

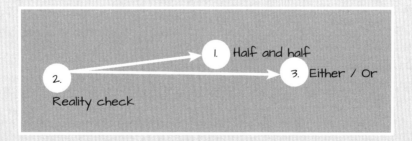

Establish Links with Space 3 (Either/Or)

And now, what do you know here?

"I still can't see it *[the topic]* from here, but I know it's there now, and I can't lose awareness of that whole structure any more. It's like having the outside facing me. And it doesn't feel like Either/Or now. It's more of a sense of inclusion inside of me."

Earlier, James had noted that the explorer had used the spatial metaphor 'joint space' to refer to Capital I and Possibility together. He now asks:

And is there anything else you know here about joint space *[gesture to the two spaces]*?

"I still want to be there."

This is the second time the explorer has stated where he wants to go. James notices the explorer is not satisfying his own want and is tempted to invite him to enact his desire. Instead James reasons that if the explorer wants to go to Joint Space he can, and continues with:

And return to one of the other spaces.

Lewis goes to Half and Half. "I just need to have a little pause in Half and Half. I have to honour this space."

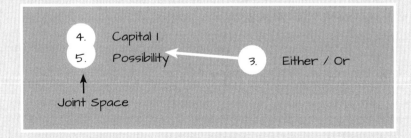

Establish Links with Space 1 (Half and Half)

And now what do you know here?

"It feels significant. I couldn't just step over it. I had to come here and make a decision to go there *[gesture to Possibility]*."

Before James can ask anything else ...

The explorer moves to Possibility and while gesturing, says, "I'm imagining a line connecting all the Post-its except Global Awareness. I'm standing on that line and my topic is directly in front of me; I am perpendicular to it."

Lewis is now clearly integrating the whole network and this is another example of a network effect that is significant enough for James to invite the explorer to learn more about it.

Attend to Network Effects

And is there anything else you know here about *[gesture along the line]*?

"There is something about that shape *[makes a "⊥" gesture with his hands]*. It's similar to my perpendicular layout that connects me to what I want to be doing."

Everything the explorer is saying points to "perpendicular layout" being an organising metaphor for the whole network. James therefore invites Lewis to keep his attention on it.

And is there anything else you know here about perpendicular layout?

"I could just stay here and relax, like a dog going round and round before it flops and goes to sleep. There is a roundness now, not just straight lines."

Having given the explorer an opportunity to learn more about the way the network is configured, James continues with the essential routines by establishing links to other spaces...

Establish Links with Space 5 (Possibility)

And is there anything else you know here about Capital I?

"It's a step closer."

Lewis takes a step forward to Capital I.

This step forward means James has to let go of his plan to establish further links with Possibility and instead invites the explorer to establish links with Capital I.

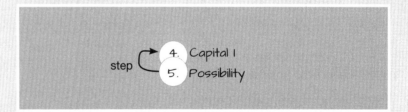

Establish Links with Space 4 (Capital I)

And now, what do you know here?

"Self-discipline comes to mind. I like going swimming and that takes self-discipline. I have to make the effort and I enjoy the results so much I want to make the effort again next time. I need the same with this, at least to start with. I need to make the effort."

And is there anything else you know here about [gesture to Either/Or]**?**

"It's not significant any more. I like the analogy of making an effort to go swimming a lot."

And what do you know here about [gesture to Global Awareness]**?**

"I don't kid myself over there. It's really useful."

Finish

James brings the session to a close by inviting the explorer to return to where he began, Space 1.

And return to [gesture to Half and Half]**.**

And knowing all that [gesture around the network]**, what do you know now?**

"This is different now. I am not here now. I'm there [points at Capital I]. I'm there, perpendicular to my topic. [Moves a half-turn to face the topic.] It's nice to compare how it is now compared with how it was when I started. This whole process has been really useful."

And what difference does knowing that make?

"The difference is that making the effort can be so fantastic as well as frustrating. But I'll never experience the benefit without making the effort."

And when you are ready, collect up your paper and Post-it Notes.

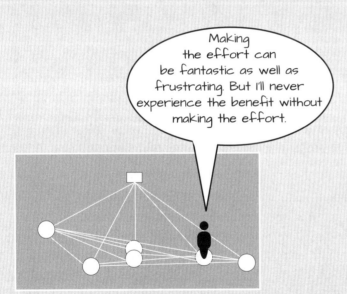

A note from Lewis two years later...

"It's been two years since the Clean Space session where my topic was to be able to create more work-life balance. I've been successful in my career, but work was taking over my life. The more I was appreciated, the more work I was offered and the more I took on. But a part of me knew my life was out of line, and I needed more unscheduled time for spontaneity.

"Paradoxically, after the session I realised I needed time and space to notice the 'distractions'. I realised distractions were where my attention naturally went. The 'I' was like the needle on a compass that could notice other opportunities or ways of doing things – and still stay on course.

"So now I make the effort to say 'no' to increased busyness, and 'yes' to creative distractions. The external success of my Clean Space session has been reflected in the gradual creation of empty spaces in my diary. The internal measure of success was (and continues to be) the choice I now have about what happens in that space."

Note that James did not know Lewis's topic was work-life balance – and he didn't need to know in order to do a good job of facilitating him.

Simple can be harder than complex. You have to work hard to get your thinking clean to make it simple. But it's worth it in the end, because once you get there, you can move mountains.

STEVE JOBS

Chapter 3

How to Run the Process

CLEAN SPACE GUIDELINES

The operating principles that guide a Clean Space facilitator are about keeping yourself out of the process, keeping the explorer's attention on their emerging network, keeping the process flowing and letting go of much of what is generally expected of a facilitator. These principles work together to encourage conditions in which the explorer's creativity can flourish.

Some people call this 'egoless' facilitation. While we understand the sentiment, not having an ego is probably beyond the development of most of us. You can be an excellent Clean Space facilitator *and* have your own thoughts and feelings – as long as you keep them to yourself. The precise wording of the questions and directions will help to keep you from intruding into the explorer's world. This is why we say 'stick to the process' – and that means trusting the process will do its job without the need for further intervention.

To assist you learning to facilitate with the essential routines we have grouped a number of guidelines under four headings:

➤ Keep it Clean

➤ Keep it Spatial

➤ Keep the Process Going

➤ Let Go

These are particularly important when an explorer does something that's not in the script. At these times, those new to Clean Space can feel like they need to *do* something special, whereas the general rule is to stick as close to the process as you can. The following pages give practical advice about how to handle the most common off-script occurrences and in Chapter 5 we introduce other ways to utilise the unexpected, incorporate the serendipitous and allow the space to become your co-facilitator.

First, a brief word about the function of the questions in the essential routines.

Written statements or drawings are the usual way to start. However, since we rarely refer to the topic, anything that has significance for the explorer can be used – an object (such as a photograph or ornament), something created for the activity, or even a perception (imagined or remembered).

The start routine invites the explorer to decide on a place for the topic and a place for him or herself. By making these decisions they take ownership of the space and their body starts to form spontaneous, out-of-awareness relationships with the surroundings.

The first two questions within the Establish Spaces routine are designed to invite the explorer to attend to what they know in a new space, what they know about their topic and to prepare them for naming that space.

And what do you know here?

supports the individuation of the space. It suggests knowledge 'here' may be different to knowledge elsewhere. Whatever the answer, the information will be associated with this space and its unique perspective. The 'here' in the question has done its job.

And is there anything else you know here about that *[gesture to the topic]*?

directs attention to 'that' (over there) while the 'here' continues to emphasise the primacy of the current location. The location of 'that' can be emphasised by pointing to it and by adding 'there'.

Sometimes the response to the first question is information about the topic. If this happens, you can vary the second question:

And is there anything else you know here *[gesture to 'here']*?

Either way, after two questions continue with naming and marking the space. Not only does a name enable a space to be referred to, it also gives it an identity and a permanence. When the explorer moves to another space, the experience can stay where it is and the person can get a different perspective on that space and the information it holds.

We do not read too much into the labels the explorer gives to spaces. Any name the explorer choses will have a history of personal associations. More important for us is to take note of the configuration of the emerging network, to track where the explorer is in the process and, as we describe later, to keep it spatial.

Moving from space to space automatically creates multiple perspectives. An explorer can never view a topic from every angle but six angles offer a lot more perspectives than one or two.

By the time an explorer returns to a space things will have happened. By inserting 'now' into the question, we invite them to reflect on the current state of their knowledge:

And now what do you know here?

Once a number of spaces exist (usually six) the Clean Space process encourages the explorer to examine the links and relationships between them:

And is there anything else you know here about *[one of the other spaces]***?**

As more and more links between spaces are discovered the network becomes ever more interconnected.

The explorer unconsciously projects the characteristics of the network out into space, and, through feedback, the network influences the perception of the explorer. Once the projection and feedback are in lockstep a

change in one is reflected by a change in the other. This, coupled with space being the most common of all metaphors, is why Clean Space is so effective.

Although the features of a network only exist in the mind of the explorer, as facilitators we relate to them as if they are as real as the furniture in the room. At the same time we aim to be in sync with the explorer but to have only a light level of rapport with them.

The facilitator-explorer and facilitator-network relationships are important but secondary. The *primary* relationship is between the explorer and his or her network.

As we explain, for this to happen the facilitator has to place him or herself both metaphorically and physically on the periphery of the explorer's network and will have to forego conversational etiquette.

Keep it Clean

Match the rhythm of the explorer

Each explorer has his or her own rhythm and pace. Some will say few words; others will say a lot. Some will be eager for the next question; others will take a minute or two to think before being ready. Some will take over their own process early on; others will need more input from you.

Facilitators have different rhythms, too. You may be a fast processor and want to get a move on, you may be slow and like to wait. In this process, we recommend you adjust your normal style to match the speed and rhythm of the explorer, which may well change over the course of a session.

Keep the process going but whatever you do, don't rush the explorer.

Ask one question at a time and calibrate when the explorer is ready for an invitation

How do you know that someone has finished contemplating and has said all they need to say? They may:

○ Look at you, stop looking around or stop focusing on one space.

○ Come out of a reverie.

○ Shift their physiology or their breathing.

○ Use their voice to signal that they have come to the end.

If you are in any doubt, wait a little bit longer until you are sure they have finished and are ready for your next question or direction.

Do not paraphrase or repeat back the explorer's words

There's no need to add any words to the questions and directions. Each extra word (even an "OK") can detract from the process as the explorer diverts some of their attention away from their network and onto you.

One of the by-products of not referring to an explorer's content is that you will have very little to remember and you may only need to take the briefest of notes. This will free you to concentrate more on the explorer's nonverbal responses and to listen for spatial metaphors.

Keep it Spatial

As you'll have gathered by now, Clean Space is about encouraging the conditions for creativity which are signalled by the explorer's reaction to their network and their perceptions. If the person is engrossed in their inner mental and outer physical space, surprised by what is happening, gaining insight or changing their ideas about something, then it's safe to say that what you are doing is working.

As well as using the questions and directions, you can encourage these conditions by considering where to locate yourself, and what you do with your eyes, your body and your voice to keep the process spatial.

Respect the explorer's space

The features of a room, the way the explorer relates to the space and the spatial metaphors they use can all take on special significance. That's why it's important for you to stay out of the explorer's way as you facilitate.

While the explorer is locating a place for their topic and a space for him or herself, find an out-of-the-way spot for yourself. Then keep to the edge of the forming network as much as possible. Only move if you have to – for example, if the explorer claims that spot as part of their network, or if they go somewhere that means they can't hear your questions or see your gestures.

If you have to step inside the explorer's network, to hand them Post-its and pen for example, avoid crossing any of their spaces or metaphorical features.

As an explorer's network becomes more defined it becomes easier to find a suitable place that is both outside of the network and close enough for you to be heard seen.

Find a spot at the edge of their network to facilitate from.

Commit to the spaces, metaphors, and the network as if they really exist

Even though virtually everything about the Clean Space process is imaginary and symbolic, the way you facilitate helps to make it real for the explorer. Use your voice, your eyes, your gestures and your body position to give the message that the network is real:

❍ Turn your body towards the space you are gesturing to.

❍ Reduce eye contact and aim your questions to the network of spaces, not to the explorer.

❍ Make your gaze and gestures congruent with the location of the explorer's spaces.

❍ Make your gestures emphatic or bigger than usual.

❍ Direct each question to a particular space.

❍ Use the explorer's names for their spaces or simply gesture to them.

❍ If you forget the name of a space, it's better to gesture to it than guess or run up to the Post-it Note. You may find it helpful to make a diagram of the spaces to aid your memory.

❍ Ask your **questions** with a strong sense of curiosity and without an upward inflection. Emphasise the orienting words, 'here', 'there' and 'that'.

❍ Deliver your **directions** confidently with a *downward* inflection. A direction delivered with a tentative tonality or upward inflection can sound like a question. This can have a detrimental effect on the facilitation since it expects the explorer to know *in advance* whether they can find a space. Perhaps they won't know until they get there.

When it works well the explorer will be more interested in finding out what happens when they follow the direction or answer the question than wondering what you mean.

Keep the Process Going

Clean Space requires a network of experiences to inhabit a physical area. Your primary job is to facilitate the explorer to establish spaces and establish links between them, out of which a network will emerge. In other words, your role is to keep the network-building process going.

In the early stages, it is more important to establish a number of spaces than to ask a fixed number of questions or to get a lot of information in each space.

If an explorer gives a long description in response to the first question in a space, you can drop the second question and invite them to name the space. Even if little information is forthcoming, keep the process moving by asking no more than two or three *Know here* or *Know about there* questions while establishing the initial six spaces.

Honour physicality

On a chair... outside the door... under the table... if there is any way for the explorer to get to a space they want to be in, then that should be encouraged (safely of course). It's about honouring the physicality of the explorer's inner world as these three examples show...

During a Clean Space session at James' home, an explorer asked if he could go to a space that was behind a closed door. "Sure," James replied. The explorer opened the door, stepped into the storeroom and closed the door behind him.

James shouted the questions to him through the door. James could only hear muffled answers, so whenever there was silence he asked the next question.

James couldn't ask him to write on a Post-it since the storeroom had no light. When James said *And find another space* the explorer appeared, blinking. James invited him to name the space he had just been in and the explorer stuck his Post-it on the storeroom door. Then the process continued as usual.

David Grove would sometimes go to extreme lengths to satisfy a client's wish to physically be in a space. While conducting a retreat in the North of England a client said one of the spaces they wanted to go to was on top of the hill he used to visit with his father. David put on his coat and said, "Let's go." The client drove them to the top of the hill and David continued the work. The client's next space was the school he attended as a boy. Off they drove again. After that, it was where the client was born. The session took the entire afternoon as the pair criss-crossed the countryside travelling many miles in pursuit of an authentic experience.

On the other hand, David employed a somewhat different approach when on a cold, wet winter's day a client said the space he needed to go to was on the other side of the street. David looked out of the window at the rain and wind and directed him to:

Go to that space on the other side of the street, find out what you know there, what the space knows, and anything else you know from there about these spaces here [points to the existing spaces in the room], and then report back.

The client put on his coat and trudged off into the rain. 15 minutes later he reappeared soaked through but with a mass of new information!

However sometimes the explorer is unable to find or get to a space they want to go to and the network-building process risks being interrupted.

This can happen when the explorer:

➤ Can't physically get to a space

➤ Can't find another space

➤ Doesn't want to go to a space

➤ Doesn't move or can't answer

In these cases, it may not be possible or desirable to continue with the essential routines. Whatever you do, respect what the explorer says – there is no need to try to make anything happen.

Next we give examples of these kinds of situations together with suggestions about how best to respond. We call the variations on the essential questions and directions 'conditional' since they are conditional on something happening with the network or the explorer. When, why and how to use conditional invitations is described more fully in Chapters 4 and 5.

Shall I tell you what I know now?

Explorer can't physically get to a space

Once you start using Clean Space it will not be long before an explorer wants to go to a space that they cannot physically get to. It might be because the space is 'underground', or 'on top of that building' or 'in Outer Mongolia' or 'inside my body'. What do you do? The easiest way to explain is with some examples.

Imagine a situation where you have invited an explorer to find another space and they respond in one of these ways:

○ That would be on the other side of the world.

○ I want to be up there on the ceiling.

○ The space is inside my body.

It is clear that the explorer cannot physically get to these spaces.

To handle this type of situation David Grove devised the idea of a proxy space:

And find a space that represents *[name of where explorer wants to go]*.

For example:

And find a space that represents the other side of the world.

And find a space that represents up there on the ceiling.

And find a space that represents the space inside your body.

When the explorer is in the proxy space you can continue as usual with, *And what do you know here?*

Or (preferably) attempt to preserve the perspective of the original space, e.g.

And what do you know from *[name of where explorer wants to go]*?

For example:

And what do you know from the other side of the world?

And what do you know from up there *[point to ceiling]*?

And what do you know from inside your body?

You'll notice that in all these examples the exact words for the names of the explorer's spaces are preserved.

Explorer can't find another space

Occasionally an explorer will wander around searching, and then say, "I can't find another space" or, "There isn't one."

I can't find another space!

If this happens, just wait – sooner or later they will stop moving, at which point you can ask, *And what do you know here?* of the space they are occupying.

Once that space is established you have a number of options. Which you chose will depend on how many spaces have already been located and named.

With four or more spaces already created you can start to establish links by inviting them to:

And return to one of the other spaces.

With only a few spaces in the network you might ask again:

And find another space.

Just because the explorer couldn't find a space a few minutes ago, doesn't mean they can't find one now. Stick to the essential routines if you can.

I don't want to go there again.

Explorer doesn't want to go to a space

Do not suggest or imply that an explorer should go to a space they don't want to visit – even if you think it would be in their best interest. You must accept the explorer's statement and invite them to find or return to a different space:

And find *another* space.

And return to one of the other spaces.

Notice that from then on each time you say, *And return to one of the other spaces*, you implicitly give them an opportunity to return to the space in question.

While these are your default choices, there is a third option. You can utilise some of the explorer's information to invite them to create a place to reflect on the not-want-to-go-to space.

One explorer had returned to every space except one so James invited her to, "Return to *[gestures to the unvisited space]*" she replied, "It's like bad-tasting medicine. I know it's good for me but I don't want to go there again." James's response was:

And find a space that knows something else about bad-tasting medicine and not want to go there again.

This accepts the explorer's decision not to return to that space, and invites them to discover something about their in-the-moment reaction to that space.

Explorer doesn't move or can't answer

What do you do on the rare occasion an explorer says, "I can't answer that question" or you invite them to *Find another space* or *Return to one of the other spaces* and they do not move, or they say something like, "I can't" or, "I'm stuck here"?

First wait and see whether they say or do something that gives you a steer on what to do next. While you are waiting you can be watching for what they do naturally when they can't answer, or when they are stuck.

If, after waiting, the explorer still gives no clue as to what to do, you can see if a different kind of invitation has any effect. For example, you might say:

And is there anything else this space *[point to the space]* **knows?**

Or

And find a space that knows something else about stuck.

Notice that the invitation in the first example shifts attention from the explorer to what 'this space' might know. The second invites the explorer to perceive "stuck" from another space.

A third possibility, if a good size network has been established, would be to invite the explorer to move to outside what they have created so far.

And find a space outside all of this *[gesture around the network]*.

There are examples of how to use this question on page 156. In the unlikely event that none of the above prove fruitful, check that the explorer wants to continue exploring their topic.

In Clean Space we do not reframe or try to change the explorer's experience in any way. Instead we aim to facilitate the explorer to take different perspectives, utilise their own metaphors and access their inherent creativity.

Let Go

Have no expectations, but great expectancy – and give up the need to know why things happen as they do.

CAROLINE MYSS

Mostly, being an effective Clean Space facilitator is about not doing. *Less is more* is the watchword of all clean processes.

Let go of any desire to change the explorer or their network of ideas, to solve their problem or to make anything happen. Instead, accept what happens is what happens, trust the process and the explorer's inherent capacity for self-organisation and self-development. Similarly, let go of any need you may have to achieve a 'positive' outcome and substitute it with a moment-by-moment calibration of whether the conditions for creative emergence are being established, maintained or have borne fruit.

Do not comment on what's happening or make suggestions. That means not adding in any words of your own – including words of encouragement. Even 'good' or 'ok' can imply a judgement that one experience is better than another. Use only the words specified in the questions and directions and, if needed, the labels the explorer has given to their experience.

Do not intervene except on safety grounds or unless you are required to respond. Although you may be expected to reply if the explorer asks you a question or indicates they are having difficulty following the process, it's amazing what they will do if you hold back from doing or saying anything for a few moments.

Not intervening means sticking to the essential routines, unless or until the space becomes psychoactive and an opportunity arises to invite the explorer to attend to a network effect. Even in these cases, minimal intervention is the rule. Selecting what is most salient for the explorer is part of the facilitator's art. In the case studies, we point out several examples where facilitators choose to stick with the essential routines, rather than address a network effect.

As well as network effects there are likely to be indicators of other types of psychoactivity throughout the session. Many therapeutic and coaching methods put a high value on displays of emotion. The whole range of human emotions can also occur during Clean Space. These are certainly a sign that something is happening for the explorer but knowing what they mean or their significance (when the explorer often has little idea) requires powers of interpretation we do not possess. Since affect does not equal effect we let go of trying to interpret and leave the explorer to integrate their emotional responses into the mix of everything else that is happening.

In Clean Space the content of the session may be in the foreground of the explorer's mind but it remains in the background of our mind. When you let go of the need to understand the explorer's content it frees you to pay attention to the configuration of the network – where the spaces are in relation to the topic and each other; how the explorer is reacting to the emerging network; when they have finished processing and it is time for your next invitation; and where you are in the Clean Space process.

The more constraints one imposes, the more one frees one's self.

IGOR STRAVINSKY

How the Process Flows

Clean Space may be a step-by-step process but it does not work in a linear fashion. Having said that, there is a general flow to how the conditions for creativity and the four essential routines work together to benefit the explorer. The diagrams opposite and overleaf depict two versions of the general flow of a Clean Space session. This can be summarised as:

The explorer defines a *context* by specifying a topic or purpose; spaces are *located* and *individuated* with knowings; *relationships* are discovered as the explorer *moves* around the network in a series of *iterations*; the spaces and links become *integrated* into a meaningful whole as the explorer has insights, draws conclusions and reflects on what has changed.

Clean Space is a dynamic process. As each new space appears, new relationships are created, the size or shape of the network can change, network effects emerge apparently out of nowhere – and any of these can trigger psychoactivity. Because of the clean facilitation, the unfolding session is likely to be a fractal of the way the explorer interacts with his or her chosen topic in real life. In other words, what happens in a session can be considered a small-scale version of the explorer's general way of being in the world.

As clean facilitators we do not have an intention for the explorer or their network to change; and we do not even presuppose that change is better than no change.

Instead, we trust that self-organisation will reveal the wisdom in the explorer's system and that (unless we get clear signs to the contrary) whatever happens is a perfect opportunity for the explorer to learn from him or herself.

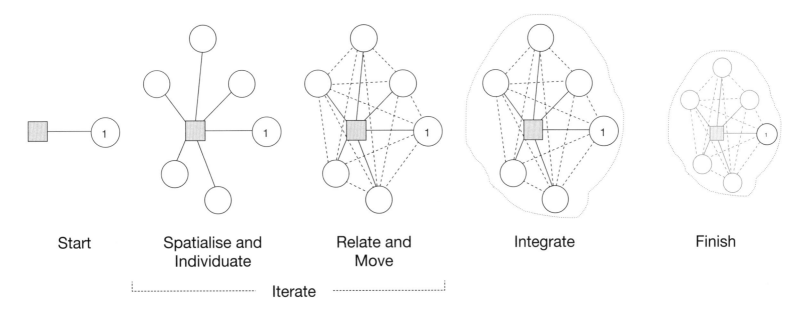

| Start | Spatialise and Individuate | Relate and Move | Integrate | Finish |

Iterate

General flow of a Clean Space session

The Ogee of Information

The information included in the network also follows a pattern. It starts small, grows larger and ever more complex, until at some point the volume and complexity is integrated into a simpler unity resulting in the explorer experiencing insights, new perspectives and other changes. The shape of this pattern: small, grow larger to a maximum and end small again – is called an ogee.

The point where the complexity stops growing and integration starts to take place is called an inflection point. Clean processes do not negate or get rid of aspects of the self. Rather, at these moments, the mind, to use Ken Wilber's phrase, "transcends and includes" what has gone before.

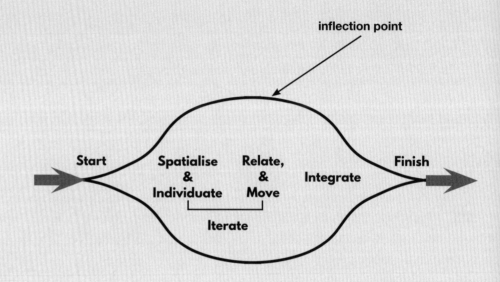

The flow of complexity over time: the width of the ogee represents the typical change in complexity of information during Clean Space.

In Clean Space the inflection point is often marked out when the explorer refers to groups of spaces, derives conclusions or rearranges their network.

The fractal nature of the process means that the ogee shape is also representative of what happens when each new space is established: start with a location, add information, add more and then identify a summary name. This occurs multiple times in a session creating a series of ogees as the output from one stimulates the start of the next, as shown in the diagram.

Over a longer period, when an explorer takes part in a series of Clean Space sessions these can also be viewed as a number of linked ogees.

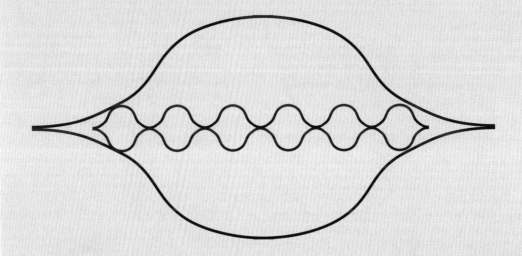

Ogees within Ogees: The fractal nature of Clean Space

Case Study 3: Knowing My Worth

This demonstration session took place near the start of a workshop with some new and some experienced participants. Both of us were present; Marian took the role of facilitator.

We asked for a volunteer to be the explorer, specifying that we would prefer to work with someone who had not experienced Clean Space before. We agreed with our volunteer – Jackie – beforehand that we might pause the demonstration part way through to discuss the process with the group. We had put the diagram on page 55 on a flipchart and had given a brief overview of the four essential routines as well as what we mean by network effects.

As the session progressed, James signalled where we were on the diagram with a Post-it style arrow and wrote the explorer's spatial metaphors on a separate flipchart as they appeared.

Start

The session starts in the usual way with Marian inviting the explorer to:

Write or draw your desired outcome or topic of interest.

Jackie writes: "How can I earn more money in my freelance business?" and places the paper on a chair at the front of the room.

Marian continues:

And place yourself where you are now in relation to that.

"I'd like to be out there [gesturing out of the window]."

This presents Marian with a choice. She can invite the explorer to go outside or she can invite the explorer to find a proxy space. The explorer makes no move towards the door, so Marian choses:

And find a space that represents out there.

Jackie finds a space near the window and the session continues.

And what do you know here *[points to here]*?

"It feels like a long way… like a leap."

And is there anything else you know here about that *[points to topic]*?

"When I wrote that, almost immediately I realised that wasn't quite the right goal."

And what could this space be called?

"Perspective." *(Space 1)*

And write that on a Post-it and use it to mark this space.

Establish Space 2

And find another space.

Jackie moves to a space in the middle of the room.

And what do you know here *[points to here]*?

"That that *[gestures to topic]* is not about what it says. That's about something external and actually it's about something internal."

And is there anything else you know here about that *[points to topic]*?

"It's something connected to the very root of me, the essence of me; it's about worth."

And what could this space be called?

"Value." *(Space 2)*

And mark this space *[hands Post-it to Jackie]*.

Spatial Metaphors

1. Long way, leap, perspective

2. External, internal, connected, root

Establish Space 3

And find another space.

Jackie moves to near the fireplace.

And what do you know here?

[Very long pause.] "Emptiness."

And is there anything else you know here about that *[points to topic]***?**

"It's cold."

And what could this space be called?

"Void." *(Space 3)*

[Hands Post-it Note to Jackie.]

Establish Space 4

And find another space.

Jackie moves to the side of the room opposite the window.

And what do you know here?

"It's more attractive here. It's warmer. I'm more attracted to that *[points to topic]*. I don't know why."

And is there anything else you know here about that *[points to topic]***?**

"It feels better on this side of the room than it did on the other side."

And what could this space be called?

"Connection." *(Space 4)*

Establish Space 5

And find another space.

Jackie sits on a chair, a short distance away from the chair where her topic is positioned.

And what do you know here?

[Long pause.] "Here I feel like I'm settling into myself. Over there *[points to Space 3, Void]* it felt like I was outside of myself. Here it feels like I am settling into myself. I'm actually in my shoes, in my body, in this chair."

And is there anything else you know here about that *[points to topic]***?**

"That it's only a short space from here to there *[gestures to topic]*."

And what could this space be called?

"I don't have a name for this space."

Marian hands Jackie a Post-it Note anyway.

And mark this space.

"It's a love space."

Jackie goes to Marian for the pen and draws a heart on the Post-it.

Establish Space 6

And find another space.

Jackie goes to the chair where the topic is, picks it up, sits down and places the topic on her lap.

And what do you know here?

"I've suddenly gone really hot." *[Pause.]* "Reconnection. Reconnection"

And is there anything else you know here about that *[points to topic]*?

"A sense of freedom. A sense of lightness. A sense of lightness and space and freedom over my shoulders. My shoulders are significant for me; they are a barometer to me."

Spatial Metaphors

1. Long way, leap, perspective

2. External, internal, connected, root

3. Void

4. Attracted to, this side, other side, connection

5. Settling into, outside of, in, short space from here to there

6. Reconnection

A Pause

Before deciding what to do next, Marian pauses the process and turns to the group:

At this point I would normally ask the explorer to name this space. But the space already has the topic in it, and so it's possible that the explorer has simply chosen to return to the topic space and that this is not a new space at all. Who has any ideas about what I could do next?

Sarah: Could you ask, *Is this the same space as the other one?*

James: Marian could, and slightly cleaner would be, *And is this space [point to the topic] the same or different to that space [point to the topic's original position]?* It's cleaner because the 'same or different' doesn't lean towards it being 'the same', and the explorer has to make a choice.

Simon: Could you not say anything and just approach with Post-it and pen and see if she takes it?

Sue: When you asked Jackie what she knew there, what came out was really a name of a space – Reconnection – repeated twice. I would be inclined to continue with the process of asking her to name the space and if it threw up that it wasn't the same, then that's exactly the information we have to discover.

James: Those are all viable options and the last one stays closest to the essential routine by asking her to name the space. If we are told something different we can decide what to do then. I also notice that the piece of paper is not in same place; it's been moved to her lap, which is at a different height. That might have some significance for the explorer. We don't need to know what that is but we can at least note the change of location.

Kim: How do you decide what's significant?

James: We're looking for signs of psychoactivity – and there have been lots. Right at the beginning Jackie said, "It feels like a long way, like a leap." That metaphor is one hint and another is the explorer saying that in some spaces she experiences more or less "attraction" to the topic. The "cold/warm/hot" and "inside/outside her body" changes from space to space are major indicators. Then there are the meta-comments, "I don't know why…" and "I've suddenly…" which are reflections on the explorer's own here-and-now experience.

All these imply that her body and the space are relating in unexpected ways. Let's see what happens.

Establish Space 6 - resumed

And what could this space be called?

"Reconnection." *(Space 6)*

(As an aside, the explorer also says, "And they are not the same." Of course, she has heard our discussion.)

Jackie stands up and places the topic on the floor and a Post-it on the chair.

While she is doing that, the process is interrupted, this time by something external and not relevant here. James uses this opportunity to ask Marian where she is with the process now.

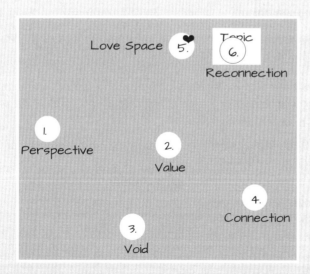

Marian: Reconnection is the sixth space so I plan to move to the next routine and start Establishing Links. I've noticed that the topic has moved again. It was on the chair, then on the explorer's lap, and now it is partly under the chair. I'm wondering whether to do anything with that, but I want to keep the process going. That is my default position; if I can carry on – and it seems like I can in this case – then I do.

And return to one of the other spaces.

Jackie returns to Connection (Space 4).

Establish Links with Space 4

And now what do you know here?

"That there are two sides to that issue *[hand gesture indicates the two sides]* so I can choose to see the one side of it or to see the other side of it. And the way I choose to look at it is the way I chose to experience it."

And is there anything else you know here about *[points to Love Space, Space 5]*?

"That *[points to topic under the chair]* has literally gone down in importance. It doesn't fit any more. *[Pause.]* It's not in physical contact with me any more."

Jackie may have misinterpreted Marian's pointing and has answered the question as though Marian asked about the topic. Marian continues without giving any sign that this has happened, although she does decide to use the names of spaces from now on.

And is there anything else you know here about Void *[points to Space 3]*?

"Void doesn't feel like Void from here. It feels like a space but it's not an empty space. It's an energetic space."

And is there anything else you know here about Perspective *[points to Space 1]*?

"Perspective changes everything."

And is there anything else you know here about Value *[points to Space 2]*?

"Value is the thing I want to connect to; I want to be in contact with Value. No, I don't want to be in contact with Value… I want Value to be inside of me. If I could eat the Value Post-it so it would be inside of me that would be great."

And is there anything else you know here about Reconnection *[points to Space 6]*?

"It's about connecting different bits of me together; reconnecting them together… They are like children's building blocks that are out of alignment, all unstable. Reconnection for me would be if they all came into alignment and were more solid."

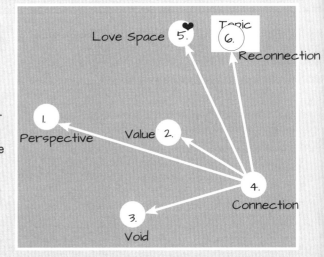

Attend to Network Effects – Establish Space 7

And find a space that knows about alignment.

While Jackie locates a space – and since Marian has moved away from the essential routines – James invites Marian to comment.

Marian: There have been quite a few spatial metaphors (gestures to the flipchart). What I am looking for is: Are any of them significant enough to warrant putting more attention on? I nearly went with 'sides'. It was mentioned twice in Space 4 (Connection) but we had just started to Establish Links and I didn't want to interrupt the process at that point.

Albéric: What prompted you to ask her to find another space about alignment?

Marian: Alignment stood out for me as something that might be beneficial for her to explore. It is clearly spatial and she said reconnection would happen if she got into alignment. Of course, it was a choice and I could just as easily have not done it. Or I could have asked her, "And return to Reconnection (Space 6)." You don't know what's going to happen when you make a choice.

By now, Jackie is standing in a spot close to Space 2 (Value).

And what do you know here?

"I'm feeling that connection with that uncomfortable place back there *[gestures to Void]* but it doesn't feel uncomfortable any more. Now it's in alignment it all feels right. It feels good. It doesn't feel uncomfortable any more."

And is there anything else you know here?

"I'm feeling a compulsion towards that *[points to topic]*."

And is there anything else you know here about that *[points to topic]*?

"It's on the floor. I almost want to stamp my feet on it… It's rubbish; it's on the floor. It's not important any more."

And what could this space be called?

"Motivation." *(Space 7).*

Establish Links with Space 7

And is there anything else you know here about Perspective *[points to Space 1]*?

"Perspective isn't fixed. It's moveable. It moves; I can move in relation to it. It's not fixed. It's not rigid. Things change… Things will be different."

And is there anything else you know here about Love Space *[points to Space 5]*?

"It's an integration waiting to happen. It's as though two things *[gestures to Love Space and Reconnection]* want to join up together."

And return to one of the other spaces.

Jackie moves to Love Space (Space 5).

Establish Links with Space 5

And now what do you know here?

"I know that love is really important for reconnection."

And is there anything else you know here about Reconnection *[points to space 6]*?

"I physically want to do that now. That reconnection. May I?"

Jackie looks at Marian, who looks back with a neutral expression; Jackie picks up the Love Space Post-it and sticks it on her chest/heart area and then walks towards the topic.

"I just want to do this now."

Jackie stamps all over the topic paper, then picks up the Reconnection Post-it and sits on the chair with it in her hand.

Establish Links with Space 6

And now what do you know?

[Pause.] "It feels different. I feel different. [pause] I'm getting a real heart sensation here [touches chest]. My heart gets bigger. It feels... I can feel its presence."

And is there anything else you know here about Motivation [points to Space 7]?

"It's a flow. A flow towards, around motivation. A flow towards it, a flow around it."

And is there anything else you know here about Value [points to Space 2]?

"The value belongs here, in me."

And is there anything else you know here about Void [points to Space 3]?

"It's gone now. It's a much healthier, more vibrant energetic space. And that's connected to the motivation."

And is there anything else you know here about Connection [points to Space 4]?

"I feel a connection here, in this space here ... these ingredients, I feel a connection with them and them with me."

And is there anything else you know here about Perspective [points to Space 1]?

"Perspective's bigger. (Pause) Like an overarching perspective. Much bigger."

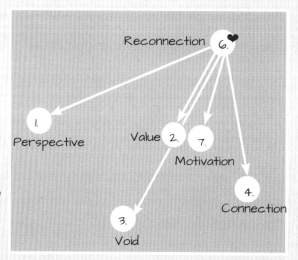

Attend to Network Effects – Establish Space 8

And find a space that knows about all of this.

Jackie puts the Reconnection Post-it back on the chair, and keeping the Love Space note on her chest, she moves to the middle of the room and sits on the floor beside Value.

And what do you know here?

"It feels solid and safe. The ground connects all of this. Like roots. It feels like I've got roots *[gestures below her]*; nurturing, nourishing roots.

And what could this space be called?

"Nurture." *(Space 8)*

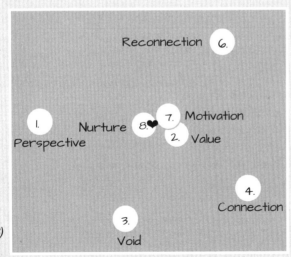

Establish Links with Space 8

And is there anything else you know here about Reconnection *[points to Space 6]*?

"It feels important. I don't know why it feels important. Something about the solidity of it and the … The eye-line between these two places is important… it's like a visual connection."

And is there anything else you know here about Motivation *[points to Space 7]*?

"This is like roots and Motivation is one of the roots. Yes, it's one of the roots."

Jackie moves the Motivation Post-it closer to Nurture.

And is there anything else you know here about Perspective *[points to Space 1]*?

"It's another root."

And is there anything else you know here about Connection *[points to Space 4]*?

"Connection is the connection between the roots and the ground. I'm seeing a tree now, and the leaves and the sunshine *[looks up and gestures above her head]*. So it's connecting the core of me, the roots and the nurturing soil, with the essence of me, the leaves and the sunlight."

And is there anything else you know here about Value *[points to Space 2]***?**

"It's pure value."

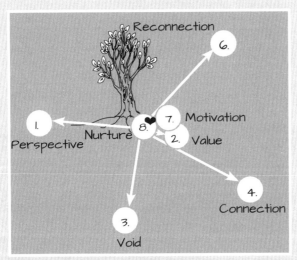

And is there anything else you know here about Void *[points to Space 3]***?**

"There's no void."

Finish

And return to Perspective *[points to Space 1]***.**

And knowing all of that, what do you know here now?

"I know that it feels great. It's reconnecting with something I knew previously and that I had drawn months ago. It's connected with that image and that's part of me. That's perfect thank you."

And what difference does knowing that make?

"It feels like an integration of all of that into me in a way that feels joined up and valuable. And that I can work with."

And when you're ready, pick up your Post-its.

Discussion

Sarah to Jackie: I thought the session was complete when you sat back on the chair after you stamped on the paper, but Marian went on. Did that feel like that was the end to you?

Jackie: It felt like it had shifted, and it could have been a stopping place because I'd moved on. And I'm glad we continued because I got to an even more valuable place by continuing. I would have had some value if we'd stopped there and it was nothing compared to the value I got by carrying on.

Sarah: Marian how did you know to go on?

Marian: That's interesting; it didn't occur to me to stop as in my mind I was only part-way through the process. And I would always go to the Finish routine. One of the things I've learned over the years is that just because something's shifted doesn't mean it's complete. It's important to go beyond that and find out what happens next because you never know what that will be and it will often be valuable.

Sarah: So how did you know then to finish when you did?

Marian: All the spaces had started to become part of one joined up network. Everything had joined together, the void had disappeared and there seemed little reason to send her back to any of the other spaces.

Albéric: She seemed content where she was at the end but you sent her back to Perspective.

Marian: One of the valuable things about returning the explorer to where they started is that it gives them a comparison – has anything changed in the last 30-40 minutes? The question, *What do you know here **now**?* implies compared to the last time you were here. There are times when it is more appropriate to end in another space (see page 162), but deviating from the classic format requires a good reason based on what's happening in the network and for the explorer.

Sue: At the very first space, Jackie's response was, "What's on the paper is not right". Was there any question in your mind of offering her the possibility of changing what was on the paper since she had decided so early on that it was not right?

Marian: It did cross my mind and our position is that if the explorer wants to change something, they can. We don't stop them but we are not going to encourage them either. When she said she wanted to eat Value, I thought, "Go on then!" but she didn't. (Laughter in the group.) She didn't stamp on the paper the first time she mentioned it, but later she did. It is best to leave the explorer to do what they do.

James: One of the reasons we encourage beginners to stick to the minimum process and get used to doing only that is to discover all those desires in yourself to help, to be useful, to ask a clever question. They are almost always unnecessary. As I have gained experience it takes longer and longer before I'll come out of the essential routines. And I've discovered that something still happens. That comes from working with lots of different people and trusting the process. I have a general principle: until you have the capacity to *not* do something, you don't have a choice. So can you demonstrate *not* asking extra questions?

Jackie: Does the space always have to be external or could it be an internal space? Two things happened that I recognised as shifts for me. The sudden temperature change and my shoulders are a barometer. Could you ask, *What does hot or cold know about this?* Or, *What do shoulders know about this?*

Marian: Yes, if you have a good enough reason – and what happened showed I didn't need to.

James: What's important is to make sure you know what is core to the process – and that's to keep it spatial. And then if you want to add one of those questions, you know you're adding it in. If you are not really sure about the core process, you can add a bit in, then add another bit and after ten minutes it's not Clean Space any more. It's some other really useful, fascinating process but it's not Clean Space. Whereas when you keep the essential routines at the core you can add a bit and continue with Clean Space, add a bit and stay within Clean Space. When you are really experienced, you can mix and match and do almost anything – but every choice to add to the process is a purposeful choice.

Sue: Can I ask about tone of voice? There are times when it feels quite harsh with a downward tone. Why not echo the explorer's tone? For example, you could have said, "Reconnection" with a slightly dreamy interior quality. Why not do that? What's the theory?

Marian: I'm keeping it neutral and I'm using my voice to put emphasis on the spaces: *Is there anything else you know **here** about **that***. I'm separating spaces out with voice and gesture.

James: To some degree you're helping to individuate the spaces so that each holds its information until the explorer integrates them. One of David Grove's principles in his early work was that the client turns up with an "undifferentiated information mass" – their experiences are all jumbled up. We aim to support the explorer to separate their experiences and keep them in the spaces where they put them, and to do that we need to use our voice, our eyes and our pointing.

We make a clear distinction between a clean question and a clean direction. Clean Space marked a huge step for David; it was the first time he had devised a process that relied on instructions. Until then everything involved asking questions. That posed a conundrum: How do you give a clean *instruction*? David gave his directions with great authority and we've discovered that being forthright generally makes it easier for explorers. The simplicity and lack of ambiguity of coming down on the end of a direction means the explorer's attention goes to how they are going to enact the direction rather than thinking about what it means.

Jackie: What kind of notes were you making? How did you remember everything? Did you draw a map?

Marian: Sometimes I make a map but on this occasion I didn't. I was committing it to memory.

James: The great thing about Clean Space is that here is the map *[points to where the explorer's network was]*.

James: Marian, in Space 7 you asked about links to two spaces and then you directed the explorer to return to one of the other spaces. Why didn't you ask about more links before inviting her to move?

Marian: The explorer had said, "It's an integration waiting to happen" and, "Two things want to join up". These statements indicate a strong network effect. I thought they were important enough to offer her the chance to enact the spatial metaphor straight away without too much interference from me. If I had said, *And join those two things up* it would have been too much my suggestion. I could have chosen, *And return to Love Space* but even that feels less than clean in this case. Whereas if I just invite her to move with, *And return to one of the other spaces* then if the joining up is important enough she will go there and do it – which she did.

James: And what prompted you to tell her to *Find a space that knows about all of this?*

Marian: A lot of changes were happening. She'd stamped on her topic; she said she felt different, connected; Void had gone; and she was talking about an "overarching perspective" – another clear spatial metaphor. I could have sent her to Perspective but I knew we were going to end up there. The whole network seemed to be connecting up and I felt that acknowledging that before we finished would be congruent with what was happening. In the moment, I chose to direct her to find a space that knows something about all of this. As it happened, she sat in the middle of her network and that space and the tree metaphor turned out to be very significant for her. But I didn't know that in advance.

Three months later...

We contacted Jackie asking for her permission to include this session in the book. We also asked what she had noticed since the session. She said:

> I had been doing work for free or at low rates; I didn't value my time properly. Then right after the workshop someone asked me to do a piece of work for next to nothing. Normally, I would agree to this, thinking of it as a 'loss leader'. But I remembered 'Value' and I wrote a proposal asking for what I knew the work was really worth. I charged a good rate and I got the work. More recently I had a telephone interview for another job and I thought it sounded like a fantastic opportunity for someone but not me; it wouldn't have used my strengths. So I said, "No". Again, this is something I wouldn't have done before. I know my worth now.

There is vastly more to the behaviour of a system than one can ever foresee just by looking at its underlying rules.

STEPHEN WOLFRAM

Chapter 4

Navigating Towards Creativity

NAVIGATING TOWARDS CREATIVITY

We can't predict the results of a creative process – they will be new and unexpected. So how do we navigate towards creative output when we don't know what or where it is?

Centuries ago, Polynesian navigators faced a similar problem. They would set out on long voyages which may or may not result in finding new lands. In the vast ocean they were guided by stars, currents and wave patterns, by air and sea interference patterns, by the flight of birds, and by the winds and the weather. They gained experience of using these phenomena to deduce when they were in the vicinity of land. When they were closer still, sightings of land-based birds and different cloud formations would help them to navigate towards the beach. These were all feedback mechanisms that allowed the Polynesians to know where they were without maps.

On the pages that follow we look at the equivalent feedback mechanisms in Clean Space:

> Emergence

> Network Effects

> Psychoactivity

> Synchronicity

Emergence

When constituent parts, relationships and interactions of systems are mapped they form a network. When the network gets complex enough, entirely new and unplanned characteristics – *emergent properties* – appear. Knowledge of the nodes and links is not sufficient to predict the new features or to foresee when they will emerge. When the internet was invented no one could predict it would grow to more than three billion users. Similarly:

○ Life emerged from a network of inorganic matter.

○ Consciousness arises from neural networks.

○ Fads and economic bubbles are self-generated by networks of people.

○ Novel ideas are born from a network of existing ideas.

Emergent properties are the result of parts integrating into a new whole. As this happens the configuration and properties of the whole in turn influence the parts in ways that tend to maintain the system. This is how self-organisation works.

Because we are brought up to think in terms of linear cause-and-effect and central command-and-control it can be a challenge to accept that emergent properties appear unpredictably and without anyone making them happen.

The effectiveness of Clean Space relies on self-organisation and emergence. Since creativity is a quintessential emergent property we facilitate the explorer to establish the conditions for creativity, and then watch for the spark to ignite.

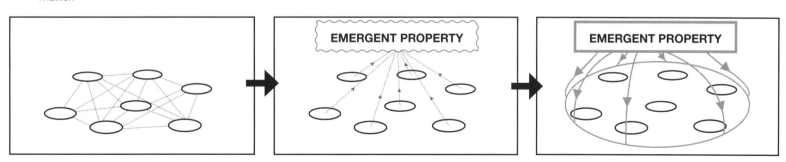

The Emergence of Self-Organisation

Network Effects

Meaning is not in things but in between. It's not in events, nor in objects, nor even in proven discoveries that ultimate truth lies, but in the process of seeking, searching, experimenting, and discovering. Behind the external activities is an internal process which manifests itself in unpredictable moments of surprise, humour, jest and storytelling.

NORMAN O. BROWN

When the configuration of the network results in emergent properties we call them *network effects.* Network effects are not found in the Post-its, the spaces, the links, the questions or the directions; they occur in the explorer's mind and body as they engage with their inner and outer worlds through the Clean Space process. Network effects take into account the wisdom in the system.

Explorers who experience network effects will often start to run the process themselves. They may move about the network of their own accord, rearrange the Post-its, change the name of a space or make a link between a number of spaces. They might say, "These three spaces are in a line and they seem to be pointing to the window." There is no actual line and spaces can't point – but in that moment it sure seems like the line and the pointing are real and that they are imbued with meaning.

In Clean Space common indicators of network effects are the explorer's:

- ○ Use of spatial metaphors
- ○ Verbal and nonverbal references to groups of spaces
- ○ Symbolic inferences about the relationship between the network, the surroundings and him or herself.
- ○ Spontaneous moving around and/or reorganising the network

When these are accompanied by a verbal or nonverbal reaction such as surprise, a comment about the significance of what is happening or symbolic bodily engagement with the network, we can infer that network effects have triggered psychoactivity. This is a sign to invite the explorer to attend to the effects of the network they are creating.

Psychoactivity

When an explorer sees the network they are creating as more than pieces of paper on a carpet, they have responses to what is happening. We pay close attention to when they indicate that their thoughts, emotions and body sensations have taken on symbolic significance because these are signals that creativity may be just around the corner.

When a network takes on extra meaning for an explorer, David Grove said the space becomes psychoactive – although nothing (that we know of) actually happens to the space itself. What we are talking about is the reaction of the explorer to their perception of the network in relation to its surroundings. For example:

Gill sits behind a sofa in a space she calls 'Retreat'. "It's nice and quiet here," she says, "but I don't want to stay too long." The space behind the sofa is no quieter than any other space in the room, but she has imbued this particular spot with her own meaning and that influences the length of time she wants to remain there.

Andy draws a picture of himself running a triathlon. He sticks it onto a frosted glass panel in a door, but changes his mind, opens the door and places it on a wall beyond the door instead. He comes back into the room and shuts the door, placing himself where he can still see his goal through the door – but the frosted glass means it looks fuzzy.

Marian is not surprised, although he seems to be, when he says, "It's like my goal is there and I can see it but it's not clear. There's something in the way of me achieving it." Even in this short time Andy has started using features within the space to create a metaphor that replicates the structure of his thinking in relation to the triathlon.

The time it takes for an explorer to start responding to the way they have organised the space varies; however most people make the shift of perception within five to ten minutes. If an explorer says, "I can't go any closer," while referring to a piece of paper a few feet away, we know that they are having a metaphorical, as well as a physical relationship with it.

Psychoactivity is an in-the-moment measure of the effect the network is having on the explorer. It is like a metal detector that signals the level of significance, taking into account the whole person – their history, values, desires, hopes, fears, etc. By noticing and attending to psychoactivity, a facilitator can support an explorer to pay more attention to what is important to them.

Although psychoactivity happens often, it only lasts a short time. It has what David Grove called a "short half-life". Clean Space aims to extend that half-life, so the explorer stays in that mode of thinking and connected to what is significant for much longer than they are used to – as that's when creativity blossoms.

Perhaps the most reliable indicator of psychoactivity is surprise. The greater the explorer's surprise, the greater the psychoactivity. Even when people know that spontaneous emergence happens, they still react with amazement, wonder and incredulity when it does. This is how our system signals the new, the novel and the creative – differences that make a difference.

Not all psychoactivity is generated by an effect of the network. Other things such as memories, doubts, desires and changes in feeling can also produce reactions – emotional or otherwise. While we honour these experiences and allow the explorer plenty of time to integrate them, we use our questions and directions to keep the network in the explorer's awareness.

How are network effects and psychoactivity related?

Network effects and psychoactivity are closely linked. Network effects appear to happen 'outside' in the space; psychoactivity happens 'inside' the explorer. In truth, the shapes, groupings and other relationships that emerge during the process only exist as a perception of the explorer. Yet it seems like they have an independent existence – which is why they can be so surprising. Since the explorer creates the network with no input from the outside, the fractal nature of experience means the network will be a microcosm of the workings of their mind.

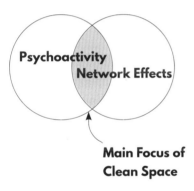

Psychoactivity
Network Effects

Main Focus of
Clean Space

Explorers generally focus on the content of their spaces and the topic. Network effects often remain in the background of awareness and may only manifest implicitly – such as when the explorer unconsciously gestures to the location of a new space. At other times, when the network itself enters the foreground of awareness, an explorer may be surprised and make a meta-comment such as, "I don't know why I say this ... but those spaces remind me of a house – a house where I felt secure."

Similarly, psychoactivity mostly resides in the background of awareness. An explorer may comment under their breath, "Oh that's interesting," or they may make use of a spatial metaphor without realising it: "I'd be sidestepping the issue." When psychoactivity is in the foreground it can seem strange to the explorer, "This is weird, I have a great desire to go back to that space."

Network effects and psychoactivity are signs to the facilitator that the process is working and is entering a new phase. They require the facilitator to make a decision: is what's happening significant enough for the explorer to take time out of the essential routines to attend to it? If you decide it is, do the minimum needed to keep the network effects in the explorer's awareness.

While we note Andy's reaction to his goal being behind the frosted glass, we don't need to do anything other than keep the process going; in this case, establish more spaces. On the other hand, if Gill doesn't want to stay too long in her Retreat space, we may limit the number of questions we ask here and invite her to move to a different space sooner than we might otherwise have done.

Synchronicity

*Chance favours the
connected mind.*

STEVEN JOHNSON

Once the space around and within an explorer becomes psychoactive then whatever happens within that space often becomes imbued with coincidental or synchronistic meaning. Sometimes unexpected things happen that can have a great impact on the explorer.

During a session conducted by Skype, an explorer was working on her dislike of her husband's need to plan and do everything by the book. She was standing in a space that represented her desire for him to be more spontaneous when he unexpectedly came home early and walked in on the session. The explorer was so taken aback that momentarily she couldn't speak.

When chance events trigger psychoactivity they can be incorporated into the process:

Another explorer was establishing her network in the garden of a retreat centre on a rather windy day. To stop her topic from blowing away she put a stick on top of it. The explorer was deep into the process when a dog appeared, sauntered over to the topic space, picked up the stick and wandered off with it. At that moment a gust of wind gathered up the topic and whisked it over the fence, out of sight. The explorer watched transfixed. Eventually she exclaimed, "That was my objective. I'm not running after it, so if the universe wants it, it can have it. I'm going to think of something else." The facilitator took a break while the explorer considered a new objective.

Phil Swallow tells the story of an explorer going through Clean Space in a public park. The explorer wanted to "discover my next steps" and was standing in one of his spaces when he turned to see a workman in a pond pulling a 'No Waiting' sign out of the water. As explorer and facilitator watched in amazement, wondering whether they should believe their eyes, the workman felt around under the water and brought a second 'No Waiting' sign to the surface. The explorer spluttered, "I might be able to ignore one sign, but not two!" Phil simply replied, "Find a space that knows about not being able to ignore two signs."

These kinds of things happen all the time, but under certain circumstances people see a greater significance and intuitively realise a deeper meaning is available to them. When this happens, they have accessed what Caroline Myss calls, "symbolic sight".

Clean Space seems to foster more than its fair share of these kinds of experiences.

Developing Your Capacity to Attend to Network Effects

Cause and effect act in webs, not chains.

STEVE GRAND

Clean Space is an interesting mixture of following routines and responding to what's happening for the explorer in the moment. Once you have run the process a few times and become familiar with the questions and directions, you will have more capacity to attend to the signs of network effects, psychoactivity and other forms of integration. This will enable you to personalise the process and adapt it to each explorer.

The uniqueness of each human means they do idiosyncratic things, which by their very nature do not fit easily into routines. At any time during the process, the unexpected can, and frequently does, happen. It's not, "Do this and this and then that will happen." It's, "Do this and this and while you are doing these things notice the signs of network effects, psychoactivity and integration, and allow them to guide you every step of the way."

As the explorer gets involved in the content, you can be listening and watching for clues to the emerging configuration of the network and noticing the explorer's responses to that network. Is the explorer saying they are relating to the network as though it's a path, a web, a bridge or some kind of container, like a bowl? Are they referring to a group of spaces, perhaps as a shape? Are they seeing a symbolic relationship between their network and the physical surroundings? Are some spaces getting more attention than others or is one space not getting any attention? Has the explorer turned to face a different direction?

When you start to observe like this you will become more adept at working with the *inherent* nature of emergence and the uniqueness of each individual's network. Then, when a spatial metaphor or something idiosyncratic occurs you'll be ready to adapt the process, and utilise what is happening.

As the explorer has responses to what is happening to their network, you need to determine whether these are significant enough for them to pay further attention to. If not, continue with whichever routine they were following. This is the 'choice point' in the diagram.

The facilitator goes through this cycle over and over: ask a question or give a direction; notice the explorer's response (especially in terms of their network); calibrate the effect of their response on the explorer (i.e. the degree of psychoactivity); decide whether the conditions for creativity would likely be enhanced by inviting the explorer to attend to the network effects or to stick to the essential routines; and then deliver the appropriate invitation.

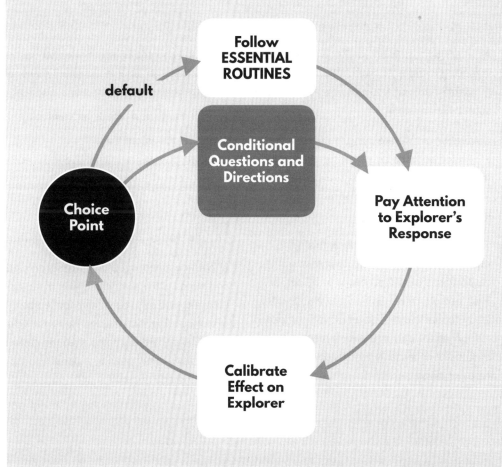

Calibration

As a facilitator, how do you know if an explorer is moving towards or away from a creative moment? Although you can never know for sure, there are signs.

Calibration, as we are using the term, means assessing both the degree of psychoactivity of the explorer's in-the-moment responses and whether what is happening is working for the explorer.

The degree of psychoactivity is relative to the individual, so the scale against which the calibration is measured needs to be set for each person. David Grove was very clear that as an "equal information employer", emotional responses are only one kind of response and should not necessarily be privileged over other types of responses.

Important sources of information for calibration are the meta-comments explorers make which describe their ongoing reactions, such as:

○ "I don't know what's happening."

○ "That is astounding."

○ "I've cleaned up my mess."

○ "It's not important."

○ "My shoulders are a barometer."

○ "It feels better on this side of the room."

A meta-comment is usually said as an aside and buried within everything else the explorer is saying, and so is easily overlooked by explorer and facilitator alike. However, when these signals are extracted from the noise of the narrative, they provide a portal into the explorer's inner world.

Often, more important than the size of any response is a change in a pattern of response. Suddenly giving a long answer when previous answers had been very short (or vice versa); the explorer's body becoming engaged in the process when before it was still (or vice versa); shifting from highly conceptual to more metaphorical language (or vice versa); all hint that something unusual is happening for the explorer.

The Clean Space process will do its job so you can concentrate on doing your job: tracking the explorer's network; calibrating their responses; and deciding how best to incorporate those responses into the process. After that, it is up to the explorer's system to learn from what happens.

If you stay clean and stick to the process then almost everything that happens originates with the explorer. Sometimes that includes them finding spaces for the less-than-pleasant aspects of their life. Should this happen you don't need to do anything special. Clean Space seems to enable people to access the troubling aspects of life in a way that provides a new and wider perspective. On the rare occasion an explorer remains in an unproductive state you can invite them to find another space or return to a more productive existing space.

Remember, the default is to stay close to the essential routines since they provide a flow to the process. However, the direction that flow takes depends on the idiosyncrasies of the explorer. Your influence should be restricted to whether you choose to raise the profile of any network effects or psychoactivity by pointing to them with your questions and directions.

In the case studies sprinkled throughout this book there are many examples of an explorer's network having unexpected effects on his or her system. One of the most challenging ideas for therapists, coaches and other 'change agents' new to Clean Space is to fully realise that in this process *change happens spontaneously*. We do not need to do anything to make change happen, since, in the words of David Grove, "The space will become your co-facilitator".

Life is a series of natural and spontaneous changes.

Don't resist them – that only creates sorrow.

Let reality be reality.

Let things flow naturally forward in whatever way they like.

LAO TZU

Spatial Metaphors

In Clean Space people use the physical world metaphorically as a canvas on which to lay out various aspects of their experience. Developing an acute recognition of spatial metaphors is therefore vital for a Clean Space facilitator.

Spatial metaphors are clues to the way our mind is organised. Each time an explorer uses a spatial metaphor they give him or herself information about the way they are making sense of their situation or topic.

If an explorer says they are 'disconnected' from their topic, it will have a particular meaning for them and correspond to a particular embodied experience. They would have a different relationship with their topic even if they used a similar metaphor such as 'detached' or 'disengaged' or 'separated' since each one represents a different embodiment.

Most metaphors reside in the background of our awareness. This particularly applies to spatial metaphors. We talk about letting people down, being on top of our work or having to get something out into the open, but we don't stop to consider the metaphorical nature of these statements. We are rarely aware that each presupposes a metaphorical spatial relationship (down, on top of, out into). Similarly, in metaphors such as 'I'm attracted to that idea' or 'moving heaven and earth', the verbs 'attract' and 'move' suggest things in separate spaces being moved in particular directions. These are just a few of a vast number of spatial metaphors that involve verbs and prepositions.

It doesn't matter that explorers are unlikely to be consciously aware of all the layers of meaning of their spatial metaphors, because their system knows much more than they know they know. There is a whole realm of tacit knowledge operating.

Clean Space stimulates the use of spatial metaphors and encourages the explorer to pay attention to them. Below are a few examples taken from case studies 1, 2 and 3:

○ I could go from here through a portal to other places.

○ Getting close to her changed how I was seeing her.

○ This is a new place to be; it's more of a global awareness.

○ The minute I stood here, I thought, 'This is perpendicular.'

○ It feels like a long way… like a leap.

○ It's something connected to the very root of me.

And Case Study 4 in particular shows how the facilitator incorporates the explorer's spatial metaphors.

How Many Spaces are Needed for Creativity to Emerge?

The last question we will address in this section is: Why *six* spaces?

We've said iteration is a vital part of Clean Space. It encourages small insights to accumulate, amplify and spread, creating new learning on the way. And it provides time for learning to become embodied and integrated in to the network of existing knowledge.

When David Grove first devised Clean Space, the number of iterations (and therefore the number of nodes in the network) was not prescribed. Spaces and links would continue to be established until something new and interesting occurred or the time ran out.

However, once he had been experimenting for a while, David realised that new knowledge would begin to emerge within a relatively short time, and that six spaces were usually enough.

As the number of spaces increases, the number of potential interactions multiplies very quickly and this in turn increases the chances that network effects will start to appear. The illustrative diagram shows that in Clean Space the likelihood of network effects grows rapidly between four and six spaces. Beyond six, the law of diminishing returns often applies and it is more fruitful to work with what has been created than to continually add to the size of the network. Six spaces creates a network that is simple but not too simple, complex but not too complex.

We recommend establishing six spaces as occurred in case studies 1 and 2 – but not as a hard-and-fast rule. You have already experienced a mini version of Clean Space in the preface with fewer spaces, while case studies 3 and 4 utilise more. Unless there are compelling reasons for more or fewer spaces, six is a good number.

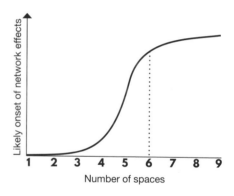

If you would like a more detailed explanation of David Grove's thinking about the significance of the number six in his work, we recommend Philip Harland's book, *The Power of Six*.

Case Study 4: Hell to Passion

Before we look at the options available for attending to network effects, here is a case study with numerous examples so you can see the kinds of choices James made on this occasion.

Start

James is demonstrating the Clean Space process to a group who have no prior knowledge of the method. The volunteer explorer, Julia, chooses to respond to the opening direction:

Write or draw your desired outcome or topic of interest.

by drawing something and placing it and herself a few feet apart.

Establish Spaces

Julia is facilitated in the usual way to go through the Establish Spaces routine. This results in five spaces called:

1. Hell
2. Heaven
3. Dancing
4. Money
5. Passion

At this point, when given the direction, *And find another space*, Julia moves to stand next to her initial drawing, just touching it with her feet.

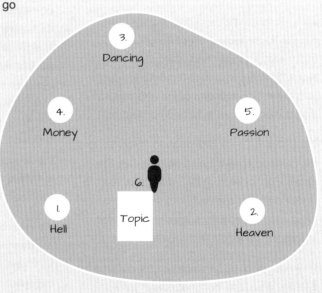

Staying with the essential routines, James asks:

And what do you know here?

In response, Julia lists a number of qualities – knowledge, strength, power, wisdom, kindness, truth, grounding, depth, joining, education, children, playfulness, intuition, animals – 14 in all.

James is now in a bit of a quandary. He doesn't know whether the explorer is perceiving herself in the space of the topic or in an adjacent space and so he opts for a more open-ended variation:

And is there anything else you know here?

A definite, "This is what I want," from Julia suggests she is in the space of her topic. Although he could have asked her to name this space, James decides not to since she has already 'named' her topic with a drawing.

Five spaces have been established so far; James therefore invites the explorer:

And find another space.

Julia moves to a new space which, after the standard questions, she names "Peculiar".

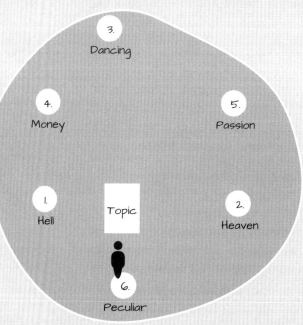

Establish Links with Space 3

When invited to, *And return to one of the other spaces,* Julia moves to Dancing (Space 3).

To support the individual spaces to become a network, James repeatedly asks, *And is there anything else you know here about ... ?* relating the current space to each of the other five spaces in no particular order.

During this routine Julia states, "I want to take a direct line from Hell to Passion, bypassing the rest." James recognises the spatial metaphor and that Julia's attention has moved from individual spaces to the network as a whole:

○ "Take a direct line from ... to ..." references two spaces.

○ "Bypassing the rest" indicates the other spaces are also in her awareness.

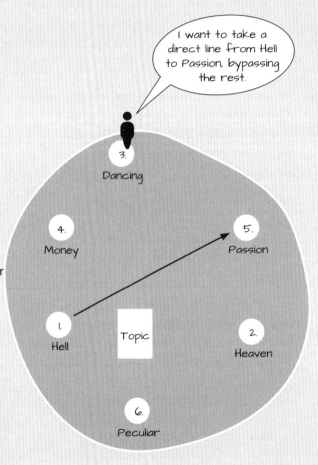

Attend to Network Effects

For these reasons, when all the links have been addressed from Dancing, James invites the explorer to:

And return to Hell.

In response to, *And now what do you know here?* Julia repeats her desire to go to Passion. This is accompanied by a movement of her right foot which looks like the beginning of a step forward. James takes his lead from this body movement and invites her to enact her metaphorical desire (accompanied by a very clear from-here-to-there gesture):

And take a direct line from Hell to Passion.

Establish Links with Space 5

Julia walks to Passion, sits down, and looks around, and then looks at James, who asks:

And now what do you know here?

This is followed by questions to establish links with the other spaces.

Surprisingly, although the explorer has enacted her desire by going from Hell to Passion this has not produced any great insight; there is little overt psychoactivity or visible sign of 'passion'. Sticking to the process, James says, *And return to one of the other spaces.*

Julia moves to near her topic and slowly walks around it in a circle.

Attend to Network Effects

Julia's unfolding process seems to be gaining momentum and James senses she is now in a new discovery phase. His first instinct in situations like this is to wait until the explorer makes the next move by stopping, moving elsewhere or saying something. However, in this case the explorer continues circling her topic silently, pausing every now and then but not settling in one place. After another circle, James responds to her moving with:

And what do you know as you *[outline circles with gesture]***?**

"Layers for protection," says Julia as she continues to circle.

James is reluctant to invite the explorer to return to another space as he's already done that and she did not take up that invitation. So he decides to wait.

Establish Space 7

One of the few remaining options open to James is to invite Julia to find a new space. Rather than trying to identify another space within the current extent of the network, James reasons that the circling and "layers for protection" imply an inside/outside configuration. Because of this, and since she is engaging with the network as a whole, James figures she may find it valuable to take a perspective on the entire configuration. So the next time Julia stops moving and looks at him, he invites her to:

And find a space outside all of this *[big gesture to the whole network]***.**

After wandering around for a while longer, Julia settles in a new space, which she subsequently names Observer.

Establish Links with Space 7

Having established the Observer space, James invites Julia to establish links between it and each of the other spaces.

Attend to Network Effects

Julia's answers seem thoughtful enough but she does not appear to find them especially insightful or intriguing. James reasons there may be value in her considering the "direct line" and "layers of protection" metaphors, so he asks:

> **And is there anything else you know here about that** direct line from Hell to Passion?

Julia responds, "It's now more of a diamond" and marks out the diamond with a gesture that goes from Hell to Dancing, to Passion, to Peculiar and back to Hell.

The diamond metaphor is a clear indicator that Julia is perceiving the spaces as a joined up network and is making her own connections. But before James can ask what she knows about that diamond, she moves to Heaven and says, "I can come here now." The "now" implies that she is doing something that she could not do before and therefore something has changed.

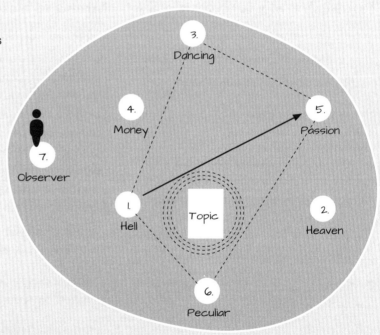

Establish Links with Space 2

As Julia has just returned to this space, James asks, *And now what do you know here?* She replies, "I can probably pick those up *[pointing to some of her Post-it Notes]* and bring them near here." She looks at James expectantly.

Attend to Network Effects

James is tempted to invite her to do what she says she can "probably" do – pick up the Post-its – but he has already given directions to return to Hell and to enact the direct line metaphor, and he is wary of becoming too involved in the Explorer's process, so he resists the urge. Instead he holds eye-contact for a few seconds and then looks towards her network. After a short while, Julia makes her own decision. She picks up her drawing and the Post-its for Observer and Hell and arranges them in a line with Heaven, where she stands looking at the new configuration of spaces. Julia momentarily left Heaven and then returned, so James uses the default question for when an explorer returns to a space:

And what do you know here *now*?

"I've cleaned up my mess, so it's OK that I'm here."

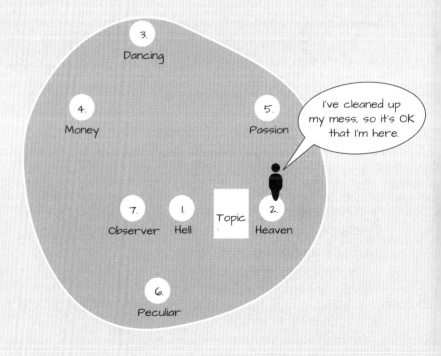

A dramatic shift in Julia's demeanour and the past tense of the phrase 'cleaned up' indicates that more change has happened and that she is experiencing, "OK to be here" in the present. By now the essential routines only exist as a reference point and James has to improvise. Given that the explorer has moved three of her spaces, and has arranged them in what appears to be a line with her topic, James wonders whether her relationship to the other spaces may have changed too.

And now what do you know here about [gestures to Peculiar, Money, Dancing and Passion]**?**

Julia responds by gathering up the Post-its for Peculiar, Dancing and Passion, returning to Heaven and placing them around her.

Money is the only space Julia has not arranged around Heaven, which prompts James to ask:

And is there anything else you know here about Money**?**

After a pause Julia says, "It's not important."

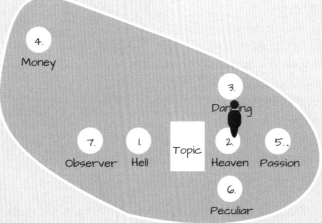

Finish

The session has been going for 40 minutes and Julia is now giving relatively short answers. James feels that she has had lots of new experiences and has come to some sort of conclusion. So he decides to bring the session to a close. But how to do that when the Post-it Note for Space 1 (Hell) has been moved?

He considers inviting her to return to the place where Hell was originally located (the usual way to finish if the Post-it had still been there) but it doesn't seem right to do that since Julia has rearranged most of her network.

Instead he invites her to return to the new location of Space 1. But she replies, "I don't want to go to Hell," so James hands the decision over to her:

And where would you like to complete this?

Without a moment's hesitation, Julia moves to where Peculiar was previously located.

It soon becomes clear why she's done this. "I've created a process," she says and begins to cry.

When her tears stop, James feels he needs to acknowledge whatever has just happened for her. He uses a clean way to do that:

And what's happening now?

"I want to present to groups. I want to be in front of people. Just like I am here," Julia says, making eye contact with the others in room for the first time.

And what difference does knowing all this make?

"It makes me want to slap myself – and to stop listening to what others tell me to do."

To honour this statement James decides to hand over the ending to her:

And is there anything else you need right now?

"Applause," Julia replies, which she duly receives from the group.

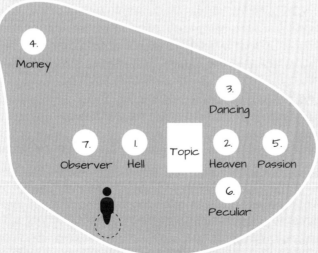

Summary

The Hell to Passion Case Study shows how a session can start conventionally but at some point the explorer's evolving network gathers its own momentum. The facilitator cannot know where the process is heading but they can be guided at each moment by signs of significance for the explorer. At the same time the facilitator's role is to maintain the integrity of the Clean Space process. The second half of the session was particularly rich in network effects. Here we list ten conditions which prompted James to delve into his bag of conditional questions and directions.

Condition	Conditional Question or Direction
The explorer occupies the topic space and describes features of the topic. By not specifying an "about *[topic]*" at the end of the question, Julia is free to attend to whatever she likes.	**And is there anything else you know here?**
In Space 3 (Dancing), the explorer states they want to, "take a direct line from Hell to Passion". To do this they need to be at Hell (Space 1). This direction invites them to go back to that space.	**And return to** Hell.
Having repeated her desire to go to Passion and with the explorer's foot indicating she is ready to go, it may be that since this is her first experience of Clean Space she does not realise it's OK to do what she wants. This direction invites her to enact her metaphorical desire.	**And** take the direct line from Hell to Passion.
The explorer is silently walking around her topic so this question uses a nonverbal to invite her to identify what she knows as she continues moving.	**And what do you know as you** *[outline circles with gesture]***?**
There are indications the explorer is seeing her spaces as a joined-up network. Plus, "layers of protection" is a metaphor that, said when walking in circles, implies an inside-outside structure. Taken together, it seems like an appropriate opportunity to invite her to take an outside perspective.	**And find a space outside all of this** *[big gesture to the whole network]*.

Condition	Conditional Question or Direction
Having asked about each of the other six spaces from Observer (Space 7), this question keeps the spatial metaphor, "direct line", in the forefront of the explorer's mind.	**And is there anything else you know here about that** direct line from Hell to Passion?
The explorer has arranged three of her spaces in a line with her topic. This invitation allows the explorer to choose which, if any, of the other four spaces she would like to attend to.	**And now what do you know here about the other spaces** [gesturing to Peculiar, Money, Dancing and Passion]?
The original Space 1 (Hell) has been moved and the explorer states she doesn't want to go to the new location of Hell. Best to let the explorer end the session wherever she would like to be.	**And where would you like to complete this?**
A big emotional response deserves to be acknowledged without suggesting anything.	**And what's happening now?**
The explorer states that she needs to stop listening to what others tell her to do, which suggests that *she* needs to bring the session to a close and not the facilitator. This question, borrowed on the spur of the moment from other Clean Language approaches, is a way to bring attention into the present and to check under what conditions the explorer will be ready to complete the session.	**And is there anything else you need right now?**

The ten conditional invitations in this case study have illustrated some of the options open to facilitators when responding to network effects, psychoactivity and integration. Next we review a much wider range of circumstances that can prompt a facilitator to employ these and other conditional questions and directions.

Creativity requires asking genuine questions, those to which an answer is not already known. Questions function as open-handed invitations to creativity, calling forth that which doesn't yet exist.

MARILEE GOLDBERG

Chapter 5

Conditional Questions and Directions

Conditional Questions and Directions

We have said a lot about network effects, what they are and how important it is to notice them. Having noticed, you need to calibrate the degree of psychoactivity in order to select which effects to invite the explorer to attend to. But you cannot know in advance if doing this will be of benefit. This is where the artistry of facilitating Clean Space comes in. Rather than trying to second-guess the unknowable, it is easier and usually more effective to focus on encouraging the conditions for creativity and to leave the explorer's system to do the rest.

In the pages that follow we map out a range of network effects that commonly occur during Clean Space, building up to a complete model on page 161. For each condition we give examples of questions and directions used to invite an explorer to attend to what is happening. We recommend that, rather than use conditional questions and directions

formulaically, you get a general idea of how they function.

Then you will be able to work out how to utilise what is happening *and* keep the process flowing. As with any artistic endeavour, becoming accomplished will take practice.

To help you understand the sometimes subtle differences between options, we have provided examples of where they appear in the case studies. There is also a summary listing on pages 164–165.

Let's start by considering: How do the *conditional* questions and directions differ from those in the essential routines?

Not very much, as it happens. They are, in the main, adapted versions that have been tweaked slightly to take into account the particular condition that has arisen.

The majority of conditional questions and directions belong to one of the categories we have already been using:

○ Know here

○ Know about there

○ Update knowing

○ Locate space

○ Return to space.

Adapting the invitations we already have is sufficient. There is no need to do something completely different. The simplest way to invite an explorer to attend to a network effect is to ask the following question of a spatial metaphor, a relationship between spaces, a group of spaces or even the whole network:

And is there anything else you know here about *[network effect]***?**

This is used in Case Study 2 when Lewis describes a "perpendicular layout that connects me to what I want to be doing" and James asks:

And is there anything else you know here about perpendicular layout?

When you decide that a network effect is significant enough to invite the explorer to pay attention to it, what you do depends on whether they have just arrived in a space or whether they have already answered a question in that space.

Whenever an explorer arrives in a space, either of their own choosing or because you invited them to go there, your first thought will be to facilitate them to find out what they know. Your choices are to invite the explorer to:

➤ Know here

➤ Know about there

➤ Update knowing.

Facilitator's choice after explorer arrives in a space

Know Here	Know About There	Update Knowing

Once that has happened you have a further option: continue with more knowing questions or use a direction to invite the explorer to move. If it is the latter you again have three options:

➤ Locate a new space

➤ Return to a space

➤ Move in another direction.

The 'move in another direction' is a new category, which we'll discuss in more detail later. For now we'll begin, appropriately enough, with the Start routine. Then we'll examine conditional questions about knowing, then conditional directions which invite the explorer to move, and end with variations to the Finish routine.

Facilitator's choice to invite explorer to:

STAY

MOVE

| Know Here | Know About There | Update Knowing | Locate New Space | Return to a Space | Another Direction |

Conditional Questions

Conditional Directions

During the Start Routine

Calibrating psychoactivity and deciding whether to use any of the conditional questions or directions begins as soon as the session starts.

A special case can occur right at the beginning when you invite the explorer to place their topic and him or herself. Once you have given the two initial *Locate Space* directions...

Place that *[topic]* **where it needs to be.**

Place yourself where you are now in relation to *[topic]***.**

... watch to see what happens.

If the explorer seems to be ready for whatever is going to happen next, continue in the usual way by asking, *And what do you know here?*

If they are looking at you, gesture to the space they are occupying as you say the word 'here'. This will help to direct their attention away from you and to the space they are in.

If they look as though they are deep in thought, wait and see what happens.

If they move or adjust their position or that of their topic, wait for as long as it takes for them to settle. Every slight adjustment is an indication that their position, the position of their topic, the relationship between these two and their relationship with the physical environment are having an effect. The space is already becoming psychoactive.

If the explorer repeatedly adjusts the position of the topic or doesn't seem to settle you can invite them to attend to what's happening by using an Extended Clean Start.

The Extended Clean Start forms part of David Grove's suite of Emergent Knowledge processes. It is designed to encourage an explorer to attend closely to the attributes of the placement of the topic and him or herself: location, distance, height, direction and angle.

The following questions invite people to experience the 3D nature of space and they may be more inclined to position themselves and their topics at different heights and angles.

Extended Clean Start

Are you ...

... in the right place?

... at the right distance?

... at the right height?

... at the right angle?

... facing the right direction?

And is that *[topic]* **...**

... in the right place?

... at the right distance?

... at the right height?

... at the right angle?

... facing the right direction?

And is that the right distance between you and that?

Ask enough of the Extended Clean Start questions to ensure that the configuration of the explorer, their topic and the space between is 'just right'. Sometimes this only takes a minute, at other times it can take much longer with the explorer making dozens of adjustments. Only then do you continue with the remainder of the Start routine.

There is no set order for asking these questions. You can ask them in the order listed or you can ask the questions in pairs:

> **Are you in the right place?**
>
> **And is that in the right place?**

Sometimes explorers respond to these questions with small positional adjustments, and sometimes they completely change the arrangement of their topic and themselves before nodding or saying 'yes'.

In a recent session with Marian, an explorer first positioned himself facing his topic, but seemed far from settled so Marian asked *Are you in the right place?* He turned his body away from the topic. *Are you at the right distance?* He moved away and stood by a chair. *Are you at the right height?* He sat on a chair looking over his shoulder at his topic. *At the right angle?* He got up, put a screen between himself and his topic and sat down again, this time looking in the opposite direction. *Are you facing the right direction?* "Yes" he said, visibly relaxing. Marian took this as her cue to ask the regular Start routine question, *And what do you know here?* He replied, "I'm avoiding it."

You need to calibrate the explorer: Do they seem like they are settled and ready to carry on, or is the configuration not quite right?

An Extended Clean Start encourages the relationship between the explorer, their topic and the space to become psychoactive from the outset. Some facilitators begin every session this way. However, if time is limited, every minute spent on getting the positioning just right will be a minute less available for attending to other network effects, which tend to happen later in the session.

A care worker made use of the Extended Clean Start with a client who had suffered a stroke, was paralysed and had very limited speech. When she wheeled him into a room she placed him in what she thought was a good position.

She would then ask, *Are you facing in the right direction? Are you at the right distance?* etc., and would use the client's grunts and head movements to make adjustments. Once satisfied with his position, she could repeat the process to find the best placement for the TV, family photos and other items.

Until he recovered more of his motor and language skills the client had little ability to influence his life. With the Extended Clean Start at least he had a say in being in the place of his choice.

An Extended Clean Start can be seen on Shaun Hotchkiss and Chris Grimsley's DVD, *An Introduction to Clean Space.*

Know Here

I wasn't expecting that!

Whenever an explorer arrives at a new space, unless they spontaneously start speaking, your first question will almost always be, *And what do you know here?* This establishes the here-ness of the space and that it contains particular information.

Until a number of spaces have been established, do not keep the explorer in one space for too long: two or three questions per space is usually enough.

If the explorer is returning to an existing space, the first thing to do – since much might have happened since they were last here – is to invite them to update their knowing:

And now what do you know here?

While you will usually continue with the Establish Links routine, sometimes signs of psychoactivity suggest the action is taking place in the space the explorer is currently occupying. These signals can be reports from the explorer of:

❍ Surprise at how they are reacting

❍ An insight, conclusion or decision

❍ A psychoactive metaphor to describe him or herself or their situation

❍ Unexpected body sensations.

A variation that can be useful under these circumstances is:

And is there anything else you know here?

The importance of surprise as an indicator of psychoactivity cannot be over emphasised since surprise suggests that something new has just occurred.

If you are lucky, the explorer will give you a clue by commenting on what just happened, e.g.:

"I wasn't expecting …"

"I've just noticed …"

"That's weird but …"

"Ah, I see the problem now …"

"Oh, it looks completely different from here."

"It's like this feeling is running up my back."

These are indicators that the process is working and the general rule is to do as little as possible. The relationship between the explorer and their network is taking on a life of its own and you can support that by keeping out of the way. Give the explorer plenty of time to be with what has surprised them and for it to have an effect. Then invite their attention to stay within the space where the surprising effects are occurring.

At times explorers imply they are not the source of the information:

❍ "This is a problematic space."

❍ "Here opens up all sorts of possibilities."

❍ "This is a stimulating spot."

These are ideal times to make use of:

And what does this space know?

And is there anything else this space knows?

A note about 'this space' questions

A note about 'this space' questions

You may be wondering about questions such as:

And what does <u>this space</u> know?

And is there anything else <u>this space</u> knows?

And what does <u>this space</u> know about *[topic/space/link/group/network]***?**

We encourage you to experiment with asking these questions because some people answer space-knowing questions with different information to questions that address the explorer's 'you':

And what do <u>you</u> know here?

And is there anything else <u>you</u> know here?

And what do <u>you</u> know here about … ?

Explorer apparently steps out of a space

Sometimes an explorer takes a step forward, sideways or backward often without fully realising what they have just done. If it seems the step might symbolise a move to a separate space, you can invite them to attend to the potential new space – as long as you do it immediately after it happens. The essential routine question, *And what do you know here?* with an emphasis on 'here' will work in most circumstances. The explorer in Case Study 2 (Gaining a Global Awareness) inadvertently steps out of his fourth space, Capital I, thereby creating a fifth space, which he calls Possibility. In this case the facilitator is able to continue with the regular Establish Spaces routine.

However, if it appears the explorer is completely unaware they have moved you can ask:

And what does *this space* know *[point to the new space]***?**

If the explorer regards it as a new space, establish its existence by inviting the explorer to name and mark the space.

If the explorer does not regard it as a new space or they do not seem interested in the new space, drop the idea and continue with whichever routine you were using before.

Explorer keeps moving

Sometimes when you ask an explorer, *And find another space* they set off as usual but for some reason (that you may never know) they do not seem to arrive anywhere; they just keep moving. In these cases, *And what do you know here?* may not make much sense, so what can you do?

Generally speaking the best policy is to wait until they do stop, when the question becomes appropriate again. Shaun Hotchkiss tells a story about how he invited an explorer to place their topic and she wandered around for a full 25 minutes looking for somewhere to place it. She then announced, "There is nowhere for this to go," before revealing that her topic was 'Clutter' and that this activity had given her all the insight she needed.

If you're not as patient as Shaun, you can ask as James did in Case Study 4:

And what do you know as you *[gesture pathway of movement]*?

You can continue with either or both:

And is there anything else you know as you *[gesture pathway of movement]*?

And as you *[gesture pathway of movement]*, **is there anything else you know about** *[topic/space/link/network]*?

At some point invite the explorer to return to one of the other spaces and follow with:

And what do you know here about *[gesture pathway of movement]*?

If the explorer gives a name or metaphor for the moving, such as, 'streaming' or 'going round in circles' use their words to reference what is happening. Imagine an explorer who is walking around haphazardly and who says:

Explorer:	Moving randomly feels right.
Facilitator:	**And is there anything else you know as you're** moving randomly**?**

Then...

Facilitator:	**And as you're** moving randomly **is there anything else you know about** *[gesture to their topic or an existing space]*?

And then...

Facilitator:	**And return to one of the other spaces.**

And then...

Facilitator:	**And what do you know here about** moving randomly *[gesture pathway of the explorer's movements]*?

Know About There

The complement to *Know here* is *Know about there*. While 'here' is a unique place, 'there' can be any of a hierarchy of spaces referenced by the explorer, from a single node up to the whole network.

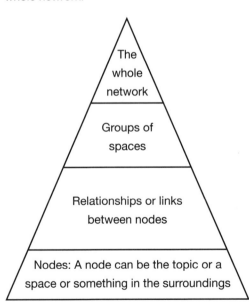

The whole network

Groups of spaces

Relationships or links between nodes

Nodes: A node can be the topic or a space or something in the surroundings

When the space becomes psychoactive and network effects start to appear, you can use the same *Know about there* question from the essential routines to ask about a link, a group of spaces or the whole network:

> **And is there anything else you know here about** *[link/group/network]***?**

You can also make use of the idea that the space may know something:

> **And is there anything else this space knows about** *[topic/space/link/network]***?**

Once a network has been established, the general rule is to incorporate the highest level in the hierarchy into your questions. The aim is to keep the highest level in their awareness as the process unfolds. In this way, the wisdom in the larger system is more overtly involved.

Explorer refers to a relationship between spaces

If the explorer has named a relationship between two spaces and it seems significant to them, just use that name:

> **And is there anything else you know here about the** conflict **between there and there?**

> **And is there anything else this space knows about** Forgiveness getting closer?

Sometimes the relationship is implied or indicated indirectly. For example, they might say, "That's *[point to space]* five years' time and there's *[point to space]* ten years' time."

It's a fair bet the explorer regards these two spaces as in some way related, so you can legitimately ask:

And is there anything else you know here about five years' time **and** ten years' time**?**

or

And what's between five years' time **and** ten years' time**?**

Occasionally, a link will be referenced nonverbally. The explorer might wave their hand between the spaces, or point to both spaces at the same time. In these cases, make use of the nonverbal as best you can:

And what's between [overtly wave your hand between the same two space]**?**

or

And is there anything this space knows about [point to both the referenced spaces]**?**

Explorer refers to all or part of the network

"I'm imagining a line connecting all the Post-its except Global Awareness. I'm standing on that line and my topic is directly in front of me; I am perpendicular to it."

"Those spaces remind me of my childhood, while these represent adulthood."

"The whole thing looks like a spider's web."

"Those are the noisy spaces."

For these explorers, not only do the individual spaces hold information, *groups* of spaces have become imbued with meaning.

When an explorer refers to all or part of their network like this, you will almost certainly want to encourage them to maintain this kind of attention for a little longer.

You can do this with the question:

And is there anything else you know here about [network effect]**?**

or:

And is there anything else this space knows about [network effect]**?**

For example:

And is there anything else you know here about that line [gesture to line]**?**

And is there anything else you know here about those childhood spaces **and those** adulthood spaces**?**

And is there anything else you know here about spider's web**?**

And is there anything else this space knows about those noisy spaces**?**

Update Knowing

The two *Update Knowing* questions that feature in the Establish Links and Finish routines are:

And now what do you know here?

And knowing all that *[gesture around the network]* **what do you know here now?**

The word 'now' acknowledges that time has passed and that what is known may have been added to or changed.

It follows that adding 'now' to the *Know about there* invitations will have a similar effect:

And now what do you know here about *[topic/space/link/group/network]*?

As well as asking the *Update knowing* questions when returning the explorer to a space, they are also useful when something in the network changes.

Explorer amends or moves their topic or rearranges their Post-it Notes

Once a number of spaces have been established it is quite common for an explorer to spontaneously alter or move their topic, alter or rearrange their Post-its or add some new spaces.

The general principle is to acknowledge what has just happened by asking a question of the space or spaces that have just been altered.

How you do that depends on where the explorer places him or herself after the rearrangement. If they occupy a new space, we recommend making use of the Establish Spaces routine before doing anything else. If they return to an existing space you can ask whichever of the following is most appropriate:

And now what do you know here about...

... *[amended Post-it or topic]*?

... *[gesture to new space]*?

... *[gesture to space previously occupied by a Post-it or the topic]*?

If a space previously occupied by the topic or a Post-it has lost its psychoactivity or meaning for the explorer then it can be ignored for the rest of the session. If it remains psychoactive, continue to involve it in the network in the usual way. At some point you have the option to invite them to return to this space and to discover what they now know here.

He had created a new space in that dustbin.

James was facilitating a Clean Space process in a back yard when the explorer picked up a Post-it on which he had written 'FEAR'. He screwed it up, opened up a nearby dustbin, threw it in, closed the lid and returned to one of his other spaces. The explorer was not screwing up the process; quite the opposite. Whether he was aware of it or not, he had created a new space in that dustbin. But how to invite it to be part of the emerging network?

Facilitator:	**And is there anything else you know here about** *[gesture to bin]***.**
Explorer:	It wasn't as hard to do as I thought it would be.
Facilitator:	**And now what do you know here about** *[gestures to previous location of Fear]***?**
Explorer:	*[Laughter.]* It feels much better where it is.

Locate Spaces

Now that we've examined the commonly used conditional questions, we turn to situations that suggest a conditional *direction* would be valuable for the explorer.

Things that can happen that may prompt you to invite the explorer to locate a new space include:

○ The explorer's words or gestures refer to a new space that has not yet been established.

○ They refer to a relationship between two spaces.

○ They refer to the network as a whole.

○ An outside view is called for.

Explorer refers to a new space or a relationship between spaces

If an explorer references a new space as they are speaking, you can invite them to:

And go to *[new space identified by explorer]*.

For example, if they say, "This is fine for now but what happens in the future?" while gesturing to the other side of the room, you can say:

And go to the future *[gesture to where explorer has pointed]*.

When the explorer gets there, you establish the space in the usual way.

An explorer may also indicate that the space *between* two existing spaces has significance for them. They will often identify it with a metaphor (e.g. 'connection', 'conflict', 'relationship'). In addition to a *Know about there* question from the space they are in, you can invite them to move to the between space:

And go to *[name of link]* **between there and there** *[gesture to or name the two spaces]*.

For example:

And go to the fulcrum **between** Home **and** Work**.**

Other psychoactive content

While we have concentrated on conditions related to space, psychoactivity can be generated in other ways. In the main the explorer will integrate these experiences during the process without any need for you to get involved. Sometimes however, the psychoactivity is of such an extent, or their metaphor is so central to the session that it must be included. One way to maintain the integrity of the process and give the explorer's experience the attention it deserves is by asking:

And find a space that knows (something else) about [explorer content].

(For another way to honour the explorer's experience, see Using Other Clean Language Questions on pages 182–183).

Marian's invitation, *And find a space that knows about alignment* in Case Study 3 is a good example.

These directions are also useful in offering a space to an experience the explorer indicates is being sidelined, ignored or resulting in harm. These often come in the form of throwaway remarks, asides and non sequiturs.

During a Clean Space coaching session a medical researcher commented that she felt "pressurised" by the Marketing Department to agree to descriptions of medicines that exceeded the bounds of current research. When James invited her to...

And find a space that knows about pressurised by Marketing.

... the colour drained out of her face as she searched for a space. Having found it she said she felt sick as she was being put in a position where she could not be true to herself.

After establishing this space James invited her to:

And find a space that knows something else about true to myself.

In that space she said she was in agony because she had responsibility for a young family and she feared she might lose her job if she spoke out.

After returning to both spaces, the instruction *And find another space* led her to establish a space she called What To Do. Here she accessed a state of clarity, commenting that she could not live with herself if she didn't raise her concerns with management.

True to her word, the researcher took the issue to her manager and to her surprise got the backing for a formal review of Marketing's strategy.

The whole network

Once the explorer has created a network and moved around it, it can often be beneficial for them to find a space from where they can view the whole system. Usually (but not always) the explorer choses a space at some distance outside (or above) the current extent of the network.

There are several conditions which may arise during a session which can lead you to ask:

And find a space outside all of this *[gesture around the whole network]*.

or

And find a space that knows about all of this *[gesture around the whole network]*.

The first variation appears in Case Studies 4, 5 and 13 and the second in Case Studies 3 and 7.

The appropriateness of these directions is indicated by the explorer using a metaphor which suggests they are thinking of the network in terms of a container with an inside and an outside (e.g. a circle or a building) or they mention something like 'a bird's eye view' or 'it all makes complete sense'.

For example:

Explorer:	It's strange... I've put every space on this rug.
Facilitator:	**And find a space outside of this rug.**

or

Explorer:	It's kind of like there's a shape to it all.
Facilitator:	**And find a space that knows about all of this.**

As well as noticing when an explorer is attending to their whole network, it's also useful to be aware if this *isn't* happening.

For example, you may decide to bring in one of these whole-network questions when:

○ An explorer's thinking appears to be unproductively confined within the network.

○ All spaces seem to have equal significance.

○ Little psychoactivity is being generated.

○ The explorer seems to be especially stuck in some kind of paradox, loop or bind.

○ It seems a conclusion or summary would be useful.

Remember, the aim is not to change the explorer's experience, rather it is to offer them another perspective from which they can form their own conclusions.

The option to invite the explorer to find a space outside the network adds an extra choice to our diagram:

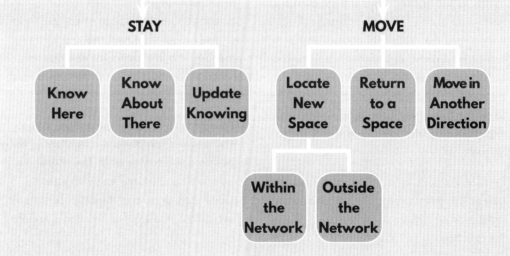

Facilitator's choice to invite explorer to:

STAY

- Know Here
- Know About There
- Update Knowing

MOVE

- Locate New Space
  - Within the Network
  - Outside the Network
- Return to a Space
- Move in Another Direction

Return to a Space

The more the explorer decides which spaces to revisit, and in what order, the better. The *And return to one of the other spaces* direction encourages the explorer to choose. However, there'll be circumstances when you think it is important to invite the explorer to return to a particular space. You are already aware of how to do this since the Finish routine relies on the explorer being returned to where they started, Space 1.

Sometimes, when a particular space seems to play an important role or when a space seems like it is being ignored, it can be useful to use the direction:

And return to *[name or gesture to specific space]*.

In Case Study 4 for example, James says, *And return to Hell*, so the explorer can enact her desire to "take the direct line from Hell to Passion".

Sweet spots

Sometimes there is a space where the explorer accesses a wealth of new knowing, or an especially important resource or where lots of change happens. David Grove called these places 'sweet spots'.

If time permits you can invite the explorer to revisit a sweet spot several times. During each visit they can discover what they *now* know here and what they *now* know about other spaces, links or parts of the network. When this happens, the value of iteration is apparent.

Spaces the explorer is not attending to

Almost the opposite of a sweet spot is a space that seems to be ignored or left out. Even though it's something that's *not* happening, it's still having an effect on the network. Perhaps the explorer revisits all the spaces except one. Something like this happened in Hell to Passion when the explorer reorganised all her Post-its except the Money space. James considered saying, *And return to Money*. Instead he chose, *And is there anything else you know here about Money?* directing her attention to the space rather than inviting her to physically move there.

Of course, if the explorer doesn't want to return to a space, then you must honour their wishes, as discussed on page 88.

Move in Another Direction

Many of the network effects that occur during Clean Space involve movement – whether that is the explorer moving around the network or moving Post-its. These kinds of things often happen without any direct invitation; the explorer spontaneously moves him or herself and/or their spaces.

Facilitators can also initiate movement with the directions: *And find another space; And return to; And go to.*

There are two circumstances which might prompt you to invite the explorer to move, either within the network, or within a space:

○ Their use of an active spatial metaphor.

○ They indicate that turning – movement in a circular or changed direction – may be important.

Enacting a network metaphor

Explorers commonly use spatial metaphors to describe the configuration of their network and sometimes the metaphors have an 'active' component:

"It's like this is a path and I'm travelling along it."

Here 'travelling' is the active part of the metaphor. When this happens, you can invite the explorer to enact their metaphor, using their words e.g. by saying:

And travel along the path *[gesture in the direction of the path]*.

In Case Study 4 the explorer used the active spatial metaphor:

"I want to take a direct line from Hell to Passion, bypassing the rest."

This meant that James, at an appropriate moment, could invite Julia:

And take the direct line from Hell to Passion.

This direction can be useful for inviting an explorer new to Clean Space to enact their metaphor when they may not be aware they are allowed to.

However, a word of warning: our intention when using this direction is to honour the explorer's expressed experience, not to try to make something happen.

Turning within a space

Soon after he came up with the idea for Clean Space, David Grove started to experiment with explorers facing in different directions. The simplest way to offer an explorer this experience is to invite them to turn and notice what happens. As far as we know, David Grove did not settle on one way to do this, so here are a few options we use:

And turn and face another direction.

And turn slowly until you are facing another direction.

And turn in either direction.

Whatever way you initiate the routine, each time the explorer stops ask:

And what do you know in this direction?

Continue to invite the explorer to turn until they return to their original position. Then ask:

And now what do you know?

When is it appropriate to invite an explorer to turn? This has to be an intuitive judgement informed by cues from the explorer. The kind of cues you might look out for are when the explorer:

○ Spontaneously turns their body a little so they are facing in a different direction.

○ Looks around as if surveying the scene.

○ Mentions a word such as: turn, around, revolve, rotate, spin, roll, twirl, swivel, pivot, circle, wheel, arc, angle, etc.

○ Appears transfixed.

An explorer went to a space right in the corner of the room and stood facing into the corner. The questions they were asked produced short, whispered responses that the facilitator could not hear. The facilitator invited the explorer, *And turn and face another direction* and asked what they knew in that direction. After four turns the explorer was back facing into the corner. *And what do you know now?* elicited, "I'd be mad to stay facing this way." The explorer spontaneously turned through 180 degrees declaring, "I'd never have believed it could be so easy to get out of that bloody corner."

Adding these choices to our map
makes it complete:

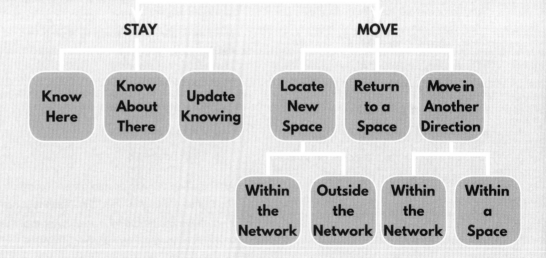

Facilitator's choice to invite explorer to:

STAY

MOVE

Know Here

Know About There

Update Knowing

Locate New Space

Return to a Space

Move in Another Direction

Within the Network

Outside the Network

Within the Network

Within a Space

During the Finish Routine

Regardless of how far you have got through the process, always leave enough time to return the explorer to Space 1 ...

And return to *[explorer's name for Space 1]*

... and to complete the Finish routine.

However, sometimes it is not that simple. What if:

➤ The explorer has moved the Space 1 Post-it?

or

➤ The explorer says they are done when the process hasn't finished?

Explorer has moved Space 1

If the explorer has moved the Space 1 Post-it, there will now be two Space 1's: the original and the current location. Since the process requires you to return them to Space 1 to finish, which do you chose?

You have three options:

○ The original Space 1

○ The current Space 1

○ Both Space 1's.

After inviting the explorer to return to one of the Space 1's and running the Finish routine, if you have the time and it seems appropriate you can invite them to return to the other Space 1 and repeat the Finish routine there.

If it doesn't seem appropriate to revisit both Space 1's, you will need to decide between them. In making that decision it is important not to be averse to returning the explorer to a Space 1 just because at the beginning it seemed negative or unpleasant for them. It is highly likely that when they return something will have changed and they will get an embodied experience of the change. This might be more important for them than ending on a high.

As happened in Case Study 4, an explorer will occasionally say they don't want to return to Space 1. You must accept that and find some other way to complete the process. Often it is easiest and cleanest to hand the decision to the explorer:

And where would you like to complete this?

Explorer says they are done

It is not uncommon for an explorer to experience a significant shift in perspective, a change in emotion or to discover a solution... and to think the process is finished. They may even say, "I'm done". However, what they are not taking into account is how much extra benefit they might get from carrying on.

Even if the explorer says they are finished, we recommend you invite them to continue. If they do not want to do that, at least invite them to return to Space 1 and complete the Finish routine.

If the explorer really objects to continuing then you have to respect their decision. You can leave the final say to them with, *And how would you like to complete the process?*

There is a telling report from Jackie, the explorer in Case Study 3, Knowing My Worth: "It felt like it had shifted, and it could have been a stopping place because I'd moved on."

However, by carrying on after the shift, she discovered, "I'm glad we continued because I got to an even more valuable place by continuing. I would have had some value if we'd stopped there but it was nothing compared to the value I got by carrying on."

Summary

The chart on the following two pages summarises the most commonly used conditional questions and directions. You will see it is organised by the same invitations used in the essential routines with the addition of Move in Another Direction.

Many conditional questions and directions vary only slightly from those in the essential set. These variations change the function – that is, the kind of information the explorer is invited to attend to. Instead of individual spaces and links, conditional invitations are mostly used to attend to spatial metaphors, groups of spaces, the network as a whole, and explicit shifts in the explorer's experience.

SUMMARY OF CONDITIONAL QUESTIONS AND DIRECTIONS

Extended Clean Start

Are you ...

... in the right place?

... at the right distance?

... at the right height?

... at the right angle?

... facing the right direction?

And is that *[topic]* ...

... in the right place?

... at the right distance?

... at the right height?

... at the right angle?

... facing the right direction?

And is that the right distance between you and that?

Locate Space

- And go to *[new space identified by explorer]*.

- And find a space that represents *[where explorer wants to go]*. *[Proxy Space]*

- And find a space that knows about *[explorer content]*.

- And find a space that knows something else about *[explorer content]*.

- And find a space that knows about all of this *[gesture around network]*.

- And find a space outside all of this *[gesture around network]*.

Return to a Space

- And return to *[gesture to/name space]*.

Know Here

- And is there anything else you know here?

- And what do you know as *[gesture to/ name pathway of movement]*?

- And what do you know from *[proxy space]*?

- And what does this space know?

Update Knowing

- And now what do you know here about *[topic/space/link/group/network]*?

Move in Another Direction

Enacting a network metaphor:

- *[Direction to enact explorer's active spatial metaphor.]*

Turning:

- And turn and face another direction.

- And turn slowly until you are facing another direction.

- And turn in either direction.

- And what do you know in this direction?

Know About There

- And what do you know here about *[link/group/network]*?

- And is there anything else you know here about *[Space X]* and *[Space Y]*?

- And what's between *[Space X]* and *[Space Y]*?

- And is there anything else this space knows about *[topic/space/link/network]*?

Complete

- And where would you like to complete this?

*Real empowerment comes from
having both the principles and the practices
understood and applied at all levels ... Practices
are the what to do's, specific applications that
fit specific circumstances. Principles are the why
to do's, the elements upon which applications or
practices are built.*

STEVEN COVEY

Chapter 6

Getting Creative with Clean Space

Venturing Beyond the Standard Process

When Marian was writing her first book, *Clean Approaches for Coaches*, she was sitting in a cafe with a friend bemoaning the fact that she had been writing for four years and it was still far from complete; she just wasn't getting on with it. To explain the problem to her friend, she used the cups, plates, salt and pepper pots and the teapot that were in front of her. She placed them in a line, with each item representing a task on her to-do list.

The book (represented by the teapot) was at the back of the line and she explained that although the items at the front would get done and so disappear, new items would appear and instead of taking their place at the back of the line, they'd always come in front of the teapot. "Why don't you block out some time in your diary?" said her friend. "That won't work," said Marian. "Something else will come along that is more important. What needs to happen is for this teapot to come right to the front of

the line today and stay there." With that, she moved the teapot to the front of the line. When she went home, instead of doing one of the numerous other tasks on her list, she simply got on with the book. From that day on, the book was always at the front and other things had to be fitted in around it. The book was published within nine months of that day.

This very natural activity employed many of the features of Clean Space without much conscious awareness — the discussion was far too interesting to think about the process.

When you understand what makes Clean Space work so well, you can apply it to other situations and processes. Marian's friend could have asked: *And is there anything else you know about [point up and down the line]?*

Once you have gained some experience with standard Clean Space all sorts of novel variations can be created spontaneously or by design. These variations come from personalising the process to the explorer and the situation, or from the need to design a creative or discovery process.

Features of Clean Space

In Chapter 1 we identified the conditions for creativity and later chapters showed how these are built into the fabric of Clean Space. While the standard process uses all the features, making use of just two or three can produce surprisingly valuable results. These same conditions can also be used to *design* creative processes tailored to a situation.

As the diagram shows, although we gave each feature a particular label, there are many other words which describe similar processes.

In summary, the features of Clean Space are:

Spatialise: All networks involve putting things in spaces (nodes) – whether those things are physical, like airports, or intangible, like aspects of a person's mind.

Individuate: Identifying characteristics of each space means they have a separate existence and can be distinguished from other spaces.

Relate: Once nodes are created, they stand in relation to one another spatially and all kinds of other relationships (links between them) can exist.

Move: Networks involve flows and interactions between nodes. These can be physical movements from space to space or the movement of attention between ideas.

Iterate: Taking the output from one process and using it as the input for the next cycle enables ideas to evolve and the explorer to go beyond the obvious.

Integrate: At some point the human mind goes beyond seeing relationships between two things to noticing connections between several things. It groups, it sees patterns, it draws conclusions as the individual components are integrated into a joined up network.

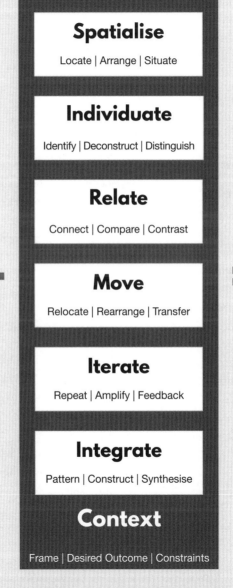

Clean +

Spatialise
Locate | Arrange | Situate

Individuate
Identify | Deconstruct | Distinguish

Relate
Connect | Compare | Contrast

Move
Relocate | Rearrange | Transfer

Iterate
Repeat | Amplify | Feedback

Integrate
Pattern | Construct | Synthesise

Context
Frame | Desired Outcome | Constraints

= Creativity

Responding to circumstances

Sometimes the environment or the circumstances will mean the Clean Space process needs to be adjusted. Perhaps you are confined to a small space with little room for movement, or to an open-plan office where conventional Clean Space might raise a few eyebrows. Maybe the explorer has limited mobility, or there is not much time available. Sometimes an explorer may say or do something before you begin that suggests it would be useful to vary the process. Whatever happens, there will always be a way to adapt the process to suit the person and the circumstances while maintaining the essence of Clean Space.

Varying the standard process will sometimes mean adapting the invitations. The challenge with any variation is: How cleanly can you facilitate as you venture beyond the standard format?

Whether you are using conventional Clean Space or any of the novel processes we describe below, keep in mind this fundamental question: Is what you are doing working for the explorer(s) and how do you know? If at any time you have doubts, it is best to check with the explorer.

Couples, teams and groups

So far we have concentrated on how to use Clean Space with individuals. But Clean Space can also be extended to couples, families, teams, departments or whole organisations. Working with more than one person opens up so many creative possibilities that we have devoted the whole of the next chapter to Group Clean Space.

Limitless possibilities

This chapter takes you on a tour of how we and others have combined the features of Clean Space in novel ways. Although we have selected eight case studies, it's possible to produce an almost limitless number of processes tailored to particular circumstances.

The chapter is divided into five sections:

➤ Explorer presents a ready-made system

➤ Explorer stays outside the network

➤ Using other Clean Language questions

➤ Designing a creative process

➤ Other ways to use Clean Space

EXPLORER PRESENTS A READY-MADE SYSTEM

EXPLORER STAYS OUTSIDE THE NETWORK

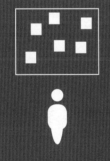

USING OTHER CLEAN LANGUAGE QUESTIONS

What kind of ... is that?

Is there anything else about ... ?

DESIGNING A CREATIVE PROCESS

OTHER WAYS TO USE CLEAN SPACE

EXPLORER PRESENTS A READY-MADE *SYSTEM*

Sometimes the explorer already knows the elements of the topic they want to work with. Perhaps they already know the:

- ○ Stages in a project
- ○ Thoughts on a topic
- ○ Components of a desired outcome
- ○ Levels in a hierarchy
- ○ Events in a sequence
- ○ Stakeholders in an organisation
- ○ Symbols in a metaphor landscape
- ○ Characters in a story
- ○ Learnings from a training or incident
- ○ Aspects of a conflict or bind
- ○ Members of a family or work team

If so, rather then start with a blank space and build up the network one node at a time, you can invite the explorer to start by identifying a space for each element, and when that's done, to place him or herself in relation to the elements.

A key difference when working with a set of pre-existing parts of a system compared to the standard Clean Space, is the lack of a single space for the topic. Instead the network of spaces arranged by the explorer *is* the topic.

When you start in this way it is as though the network comes ready-formed and so more time can be spent on exploring links and network effects. The downside is that the initial emergent creation of spaces is lost.

Even when the explorer has not come with a prepared system you can invite them to write down six aspects of their topic on separate Post-its and to arrange them around the room and then to find a space for him or herself.

Next are three case studies which illustrate different ways to make use of an explorer's pre-existing system. They involve factors of a problem, timescales in a business and parts of a person:

- ➤ My Big Problem
- ➤ Taking My Business to a New Stage
- ➤ I Came Out of Myself

Case Study 5: My Big Problem

During a workshop, James asked for a volunteer for a demonstration. A young woman jumped up and said, "I've got a big problem. Here it is." In her hand was a pile of papers with things written on them. "Each one of these represents something to do with my problem." James was not planning to demonstrate Clean Space but it seemed ideally suited to the situation, so he invited the explorer to:

Place those *[points to papers]* **where they need to be.**

For the next few minutes the explorer set about the task of laying out her pieces of paper on the floor. James watched the network appear and counted – there were 25 pieces of paper.

Once the explorer was happy with where she had placed everything, James invited her to:

And place yourself in relation to these *[gesture around all the papers]*.

She stood in the centre of the papers.

And what do you know here?

"I'm in the middle of a big mess."

And is there anything else you know here about these *[sweeping gesture]*?

[Looking around.] "It's too big. I can't ... I can't ... I don't know what to do."

And go to one of these spaces *[sweeping gesture]*.

Five more repetitions of this three-part routine resulted in the explorer visiting six spaces and discovered connections between many of the spaces. Having explored some of the detail *within* the network, it seemed like the explorer might benefit from a more global perspective:

And find a space outside all of this.

She moved to a distant corner of the room and contemplated the whole network. From there it became clear to her what was most important. Spontaneously she started to put the papers into a smaller and smaller number of piles. From the outside it looked as though she was engaged in a game of patience with giant playing cards. Eventually five piles remained which she arranged in what looked like a pentagon.

To complete the process she was returned to her original space, which just happened to be in the middle of the shape. And the difference? She knew what she needed to do about her big problem that was now manageable.

Case Study 6: Taking My Business to the Next Stage

In the previous example of a pre-given system, James had no idea what was written on any of the pieces of paper and so did not specify how the explorer should move around the network. In this example, however, there is a clear time structure. Marian uses the structure to invite the client to visit the spaces in order.

The session starts with the explorer saying, "I want to organise my thinking about taking my business to the next stage – that is growing it to $5 million per year. There are five to six stages and I need to get greater clarity on how they are organised."

The explorer is given a number of Post-it Notes and invited to *Place those five or six stages somewhere [sweeping gesture around the room].* The explorer places six Post-its and as he does he says (but does not write) their names:

- ○ Three to four months
- ○ One year
- ○ Eighteen months
- ○ Two and a half years
- ○ Three and a half years
- ○ Now

Marian makes a mental note of each name before continuing:

And place yourself where you are in relation to these *[gesture to Post-its].*

Surprisingly, the explorer does not go to Now. Instead he takes a chair and sits nearer to 3-4 months. He is now sitting in Space 1.

Since the explorer has chosen not to start at Now, Marian follows his lead and invites him to visit each of the five future spaces in the order he placed them, starting with Three to Four Months. In each space he is asked only one question:

And what do you know here at *[name of space]*?

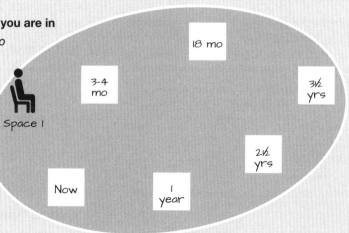

When the explorer gets to Three-and-a-half Years he is also asked:

And what do you know here about *[each one of the other five spaces]***?**

Marian notes that the explorer starts to talk about "the relationships between the stages" while pointing between the Post-its and so invites the explorer to:

Go to the relationship between 3-4 months **and** 1 year.

And what do you know here?

And then:

Go to the relationship between 1 year **and** 18 months**.**

Instead, the explorer moves to a new location (2 on the diagram) and says, "Interesting that *[uses his finger to follow the line of the Post-it Notes in a zig-zag shape]*."

Marian responds with:

And what do you know here about *[replicates zig-zag shape]***?**

"It's like they are stepping stones towards a lush green garden *[points to 3½ years]*."

So Marian asks about the metaphor: *And is there anything else you know about 'stepping stones'?* and then points to 3½ years: *And is there anything else you know about 'lush green garden' there?* Both questions produce long descriptions.

For the first time the explorer is directed to *Go to Now.*

Lastly, the explorer is returned to Space 1, where he sits down and completes the Finish routine.

What difference does knowing all this make?

"I'm more centred. More open. I feel the impetus more intensely. There's a greater stability in my legs. I'd say the impetus is two and a half times stronger than it was. I want to plunge in."

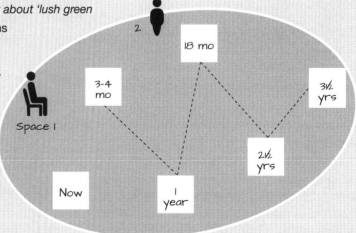

Case Study 7: I Came Out of Myself

The following transcript illustrates a novel use of Clean Space. It begins part way through a clean coaching session with James. Rather than having an explorer and topic, this example starts with two aspects of the explorer: "I" and "myself". Post-its are not used and spaces are not named. We have left out most of the explorer's responses to make it easier to see the way the Clean Space process has been used.

The explorer arrived shaking, feeling crushed and physically weak: "I'm desperate. I feel like running away. I'm afraid of not succeeding." As the session meandered from topic to topic, she again raised her fear of not succeeding in her chosen profession and then said, "There are things I could be doing that I'm not doing." This was followed by a quiet contemplation which appeared to involve extensive internal processing and a clear shift in her physiology. The session continued:

James: **What just happened?**

Explorer: *[Sitting at 1]* I came out of myself *[gestures left]*. I took a good look at myself. I'm now in a better place.

James: **And when you** came out of yourself**, and** took a look at yourself**, where did you** look at yourself **from?**

Explorer: Over there *[points to her left, space 2]*. I come out of myself and go to over there.

James: **Go to** over there *[points to 2]*.

Explorer: *[Gets up and moves to 2.]*

James: **And what do you know here?**

Explorer: I look at myself *[looks at 1]*. I hear more positive things. I take them back *[returns to sitting at 1]*.

James: **And what do you know here?**

Explorer: I feel better.

James: **And find another space.**

Explorer: *[Moves to 3.]*

James: **And what do you know here?**

And is there anything else you know here about *[points to 1]***?**

And is there anything else you know here about *[points to 2]***?**

And is there anything else you know here about those two *[gestures to 1 & 2]***?**

And find another space.

Explorer: *[Moves to 4.]*

James: **And what do you know here?**

And is there anything else you know here about *[gestures to 1, 2 and 3]***?**

And find another space that knows about all of this *[gestures to 1, 2, 3 and 4].*

Explorer: *[Moves to 5.]*

James: **And what do you know here?**

Explorer: A huge depth of love. *[Pause.]* An undeniable light, really gentle, yet passionate, and compassionate, and pure, whiter than white. Almost sacred. Closer to the divine.

James: **And return to** *[points to 1].*

And now what do you know?

And what difference does it make to know that?

The explorer gave a long explanation during which she mentioned how she would like to handle her difficult situation in the future. When she had finished, this desired outcome was recapped and the coaching session continued.

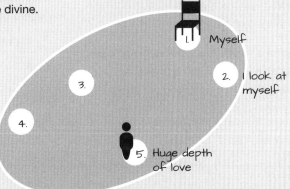

In order for "I" to take a good look at "myself", logically, they must be in different places.

James checks this assumption by inviting the explorer – verbally and nonverbally – to "Go to" the location indicated for "I".

This sets the scene for a novel Clean Space process. Once a third space is established, the explorer can consider "myself" (Space 1), "I" (Space 2) and the *relationship* between them. James continues this process, inviting the explorer to find a fourth space from which she can consider the previous three. By the time the explorer reaches a fifth space, she has accessed an "almost sacred" state, which has a profound impact on her relationship with herself. This prompts a return to the original position and the completion of the Finish routine.

EXPLORER *STAYS* OUTSIDE THEIR NETWORK

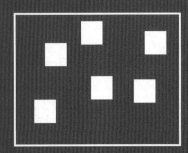

Conventional Clean Space and the variations described in the previous few pages are based on the explorer moving around *inside* the network they create. The explorer can also create a network from the *outside*. Instead of their body moving between spaces, different perspectives come from the explorer moving their *attention* around the network.

A convenient way to do this is to use Post-its on a table or wall or small objects on a table. Using salt, pepper and tea pots as in Marian's tea pot story is an example.

Working on a wall or table makes the process more suitable where space is limited or for those settings where asking people to physically move might prove problematic.

Please note, we strongly recommend that the explorer physically move to various spaces whenever possible, even it seems a little awkward at first.

A hybrid method, when using Post-its on a table, is to position it away from a wall so that the explorer(s) can walk around it and take different perspectives on their network.

The following two examples show how the proces works when the explorer remains outside a network:

➤ Exploring words in a sentence
➤ Solving a management problem

Exploring Words in a Sentence

Every word in a sentence is an influential part of that sentence. You can make use of this feature in a fascinating Clean Space process. Invite a person to think of a topic they want to explore (such a personal mission statement, a problem they are experiencing, or perhaps something about him or herself they would like to change or develop) and write a single sentence that represents that topic. Each word in that sentence is then written on a separate Post-it (if the sentence is written large enough the paper with the sentence can be cut up). The explorer is invited to recreate the sentence by placing the words on a wall or table and then to find a space for him or herself.

The basic Clean Space questions can be adapted to enquire about the individual words:

And what do you know about [point to and name word]**?**

And what does that [word] **know?**

And what does that [word] **know about that** [another word]**?**

And is there anything else you know here about those [two or more words]**?**

And find another space.

This routine can be repeated from a number of spaces.

If appropriate, further questions incorporating directional verbs (page 188) may be included. Separating, removing, replacing or rearranging one or more words can result in surprising insights. In a workshop that included this activity, one participant cut up a sentence about his marriage into separate words rather than using Post-its. When invited to *Separate any of the words* he cut the word 'relationship' into 'relation' and 'ship' which led to an insightful metaphor about marriage being a journey over the sea of life.

Case Study 8: Solving a Management Problem

James was asked to help a manager in a large organisation work out a solution to a problem. Some long-standing employees were steadfastly continuing to use an old tried-and-tested project management system, rather than switch to the newly installed system.

James asked the manager to describe what was going on. James recorded each piece of information on one of three different coloured Post-it Notes:

- ○ Yellow for the current problematic situation
- ○ Blue for resources
- ○ Orange for desired outcomes

James was helping the manager make distinctions between problems, resources and outcomes because during a preliminary conversation it appeared these were jumbled up in the manager's mind.

Each Post-it was randomly stuck on a large whiteboard. When the manager had described as many of the elements as he could – after lots of *And is there anything else you know?* prompts – James invited him to arrange the Post-its. The manager jumped up and eagerly organised them, adding a few more himself. He arranged the yellow problems in a circle with the blue resources to one side and the orange outcomes positioned on the other side. After a while he stood back to contemplate his work.

And what do you know here?

He first noticed that there were many more yellow Post-its, some blue, and only few orange.

And is there anything else you know here?

As extra information was described – mostly about resources and desired outcomes –

the manager was invited to write it on an appropriately coloured Post-it and add it to the growing network.

There followed a series of Clean Space questions, with more additions to the network:

And what do you know about [point to and name item]**?**

And what does that [item] **know?**

And is there anything else you know about [item] **and** [another item]**?**

And what does that [item] **know about that** [another item]**?**

These questions were repeated for several items before the manager was asked:

And is there anything else you know here about all these [sweeping gesture]**?**

Followed by:

And go to another space.

The manager looked surprised, but found a new position anyway. More Clean Space questions followed. At one point the manager spontaneously moved all of the blue resources around the outside of the yellow circle. There were not enough to fully encircle the yellow problems so he grabbed the stack of unused blue Post-its and added them until they formed a complete circle. It was time to find a third space.

To end, the manager returned to his original seat to reflect on his learnings.

Commenting afterwards, the manager said he was surprised how little time it took to get the first outpouring of information on the board. Then, having apparently exhausted his knowledge, he found there was much more to come out. He hadn't realised focusing on the problem meant he had ignored so many resources, especially people he had considered not relevant to the problem. He said he "played along" with James when asked to go to another space, thinking it wouldn't make any difference, and was shocked when he saw the whole thing with "fresh eyes". Originally he had seen the problem like a "snake eating its own tail" but when he "stepped out" of the system he realised there was a bigger issue: there wasn't enough dialogue between people using the new system and those using the old. He could see that increased co-operation would make things run more smoothly. He decided to make this his focus and wrote it on an orange Post-it.

It would mean the recalcitrant managers would see themselves more and more on a "tangent" and sooner or later they would join the new system of their own accord.

Of course it is cleaner for the explorer to do all the Post-it Note writing from the beginning but in this case it worked for James to start writing down the manager's thoughts.

More to Explore

It is possible to extend the process once the network has been created on a wall or table. Then the whole network can be used as the starting point (topic) for a full Clean Space session.

Arranging Post-its on a wall or table works especially well with a small group or team. The individuals can find their own spaces or locate group spaces which they all occupy together.

USING OTHER CLEAN LANGUAGE QUESTIONS

What kind of ... is that?

Is there anything else about ... ?

The Clean Space invitations are part of a larger set of questions and directions called Clean Language. Developed over 25 years by David Grove, Clean Language was originally devised for working therapeutically with the metaphors clients used to describe their inner experiences. Clean Language later expanded into a generalised practice for 'staying clean' when coaching, facilitating, researching, investigating, interviewing and so on.

Two of the many ways other Clean Language questions can work with Clean Space are:

➤ To **develop metaphors** that emerge during Clean Space

or

➤ To **establish a metaphor landscape** which is then used as the network for Clean Space

Developing Metaphors within Clean Space

We have already described how spatial metaphors are important in Clean Space, how they are indicators of network effects, and how they can be incorporated into the process. Sometimes an explorer will use a metaphor which is not spatial and yet is clearly significant for them. Occasional repeating back of the metaphor or name for a space using the explorer's exact words is a way to acknowledge that significance. There is rarely a need to use full sentences; key words will be enough. How do we know the metaphor is significant? Two clues go hand in hand: the psychoactivity of the metaphor; and the involvement of the person's body. The more they embody the metaphor and the more they respond to it with surprise, wonder or insight, the more significant it is likely to be.

Marian was facilitating when, towards the end of a Clean Space session, the explorer said, "It's like I am in a wooden hut *[marks out the walls around her]*. Bread is baking and the smell of the bread is going out the window and making a path *[gestures]* which people can follow to my door." It was clear that the explorer was intimately engaged with her metaphor and so Marian asked a few basic Clean Language questions to deepen the explorer's experience.

And is there anything else about that *[symbol/metaphor]***?**

And what kind of *[symbol/metaphor]* **is that?**

Once developed, the metaphor was related to the other spaces:

And when *[key characteristics of the metaphor]* **what do you know about** *[point to and name one of the other spaces]***?**

The effect on the explorer was profound. These simple questions held the explorer's attention on their metaphor for a full ten minutes and supported her to fully embody the image, sounds and feelings of being in this unique wooden hut — an experience she may well remember for many years to come.

Ten minutes in one place is a long time in Clean Space when one of the key principles is to keep the process moving, especially until the network is established. In this example the extra questions came towards the end of the session. If near the beginning you decide to ask a few extra clean questions, ask only two or three before returning to establishing spaces and links.

Clean Space within a Metaphor Landscape

We have already described several ways of working with a ready-made system (pages 172–177) and here is another one. David Grove's early work showed how a person's naturally occurring metaphors can form a metaphor landscape existing in their mind-body space. This 'landscape' will be composed of a number of interrelated symbols each with a particular location.

These symbols can be things you might come across in real life, such as trees, rivers, people, buildings; they can be imaginary things like dragons, ghosts, strange worlds; or they can be abstract shapes, forces, and senses – in short, anything.

Sometimes, after a person has been facilitated to create a metaphor landscape, they can be invited to externalise it by laying it out in physical space. As they do this, they create a network where the names of the spaces are the names of the symbols occupying those spaces, and the links represent the relationships between the symbols. Then the person can explore their imaginary landscape by moving around the physical network. Since the explorer has populated the space with personal symbols, the network will very quickly become psychoactive.

Corporate metaphors

Some companies and organisations have well-established metaphors for their 'mission' or projects. These metaphors can be used as the network for Clean Space. For example, if the metaphor of a 'roadmap' is in common use, a roadmap can be created on the floor. Clean Space can be used to explore various points on and off the road – and on and off the map.

This process can be done with someone in a leadership role or with a management team (see chapter 7).

Although it takes longer, a cleaner approach is for the team to create their own joint metaphor using Caitlin Walker's Metaphors at Work process (described in her book, *From Contempt to Curiosity*). The output can then be used as the network for a Clean Space activity.

For how to facilitate a person to create a metaphor landscape, see *Clean Approaches for Coaches* (Marian Way) and *Metaphors in Mind* (James Lawley and Penny Tompkins).

Physical environments

David Grove invited clients to externalise their interior landscape in other ways. Between sessions, he often assigned clients the task of finding an outer physical space that simulated their inner metaphor landscape. This could be a specific place or a kind of environment and it could also be less tangible, such as the angle of a view or an opening.

Once they have found the correct perspective and surroundings, the explorer can be asked (or they can ask themselves) Clean Space questions utilising the features of the landscape as part of their network.

For example, one person found a clearing in a wood which matched a previous metaphor landscape. They were able to explore the 'entrance', 'open space', 'dense forest', 'old tree' etc. by going to those spaces. As they moved from space to space they encountered a variety of perspectives which, because of the correspondence between the physical world and their inner world, had great personal significance.

Clean Language is simple because people are complex enough.

DAVID GROVE

DESIGNING A CREATIVE PROCESS

Clean Space is multi-layered. It consists of the *principles* described in the guidelines in Chapter 3, the *process* described in Chapters 2 and 4, and the *practice* of using clean questions and directions. Once you have grasped the principles and practice it is possible to create all sorts of novel processes, tailored to particular circumstances.

In this section we describe a range of activities generated by people being creative with Clean Space. We focus on four categories:

➤ Moving the topic

➤ Adding directional verbs

➤ Using an existing model or metaphor

➤ Importing Clean Space into other methods

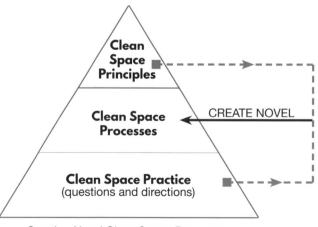

Creating Novel Clean Space Processes

Moving the Topic

So far we have described the various ways an explorer can create a network and move around *within* it, and how they can create a network from the *outside* and move the Post-its or objects around. David Grove experimented with another variation — moving the topic. There are several versions of this process. The following is ours.

Use the standard Start routine to position the topic and the explorer. Facilitate the explorer to go through the following routine a further five times:

And find another space for that *[topic]***.**

When the topic has been repositioned, the explorer will either return to their original position where they can be asked:

And now what do you know here?

And what does that *[topic]* **know there?**

Or they will find a new space:

And what do you know here?

And what does that *[topic]* **know there?**

After five iterations of moving the topic and asking *the same* questions, complete the process with:

And return that *[topic]* **to its starting space.**

And return to *[where explorer started]***.**

And now what do you know?

And what difference does knowing that make?

Another variation involves the explorer recording their answers at each iteration on the topic sheet. In this version the explorer starts with a large sheet of paper or a bunch of Post-its which they can stick on the topic sheet.

The process starts with the usual positioning of the topic and the explorer, followed by:

And what does that *[topic]* **know?**

And put that *[the response]* **on there** *[point to topic]***.**

Either invite the topic (or the explorer or both) to *Find another space* and repeat this question and these directions five more times. Then finish as above.

These variations usually take less time than a full Clean Space process and in the last example the explorer ends up with a written record of their answers. Although these variations are simple to facilitate they can be surprisingly effective in generating emergent knowledge, creative insights and novel solutions. However, what they gain in time and simplicity they lose in network linking and especially responding to network effects.

Adding Directional Verbs

Clean Space is based on the metaphor that physical space can have psychological and symbolic meaning. For example, in the essential directions several physical actions can also be interpreted metaphorically:

○ Place

○ Find

○ Return to

And similarly in the conditional directions:

○ Go to

○ Turn

This gave us an idea. What other actions could be brought into Clean Space?

While there are hundreds of action words (verbs), only a few are neutral enough to be considered clean in some circumstances (because they do not specify *the way* they are to be enacted). These include:

○ Move

○ Remove

○ Separate

○ Bring together

○ Raise

○ Lower

These words can be inserted in the following directions and questions:

And *** any of the** *[Post-its]***.**

And can any of the other *[Post-its]* **be *****ed ?**

For example:

And move any of the *[Post-its]***.**

And can any of the other *[Post-its]* **be moved ?**

The example on page 179 illustrates how directional verbs were used in a personal development workshop activity.

We do not recommend using these directions in conventional Clean Space unless the explorer says or does something that indicates the action will be congruent with his or her network and metaphors. The main reason: these words add complexity and the process works fine without them. Instead we recommend reserving these directional verbs for discovery or creative workshops.

Using an Existing Model or Metaphor

So far we have discussed extending Clean Space by small degrees, varying the protocol and adding directional verbs. Now we look at how other problem solving, creativity, action planning and self-development models can be incorporated into a Clean Space-style process.

Some models can easily be utilised because they already make use of spatial metaphors. For example, those that involve steps, stages, phases or levels: the Dreyfus Model of Skill Acquisition; Prochaska, Norcross & Diclemente's Six Stages of Change; Tuckman's Team Formation; and the Karpman Drama Triangle, to name but a few.

Similarly, any models that involve a quadrant can easily be spatialised: Ken Wilber's Integral Model; Kolb's Learning Cycle; and the Johari Window for example.

In fact, almost any model is open to its parts being placed on a floor (spatialise), an explorer discovering what they know at each space (individuate), moving from space to space, relating the parts, cycling round more than once (iterate), and coming to some overall learning or conclusion (integrate).

Clean Space and existing models can be used in two ways. If the explorer knows the model it can be used as a coaching, problem solving or creativity tool. If the model is not known, it can become a means for the explorer to understand the model and especially the distinction between the parts. The latter is particularly effective when a team or small learning group occupy the spaces together.

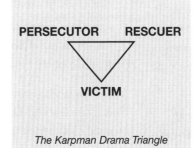

PRECONTEMPLATION
CONTEMPLATION
PREPARATION
ACTION
MAINTENANCE
TRANSCENDENCE

*Six Stages of Change -
Prochaska, Norcross & Diclemente*

EXPERT
PROFICIENT
COMPETENT
BEGINNER
NOVICE

*The Dreyfus Model of Skill
Acquisition*

PERSECUTOR   RESCUER

VICTIM

The Karpman Drama Triangle

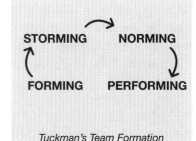

STORMING   NORMING

FORMING   PERFORMING

Tuckman's Team Formation

Case Study 9:
The Fragile-Robust-Growth Spectrum

Ken Smith was working with a senior manager who wanted to find a creative way to engage her staff in the change agenda of her organisation. One of the key components of managing the change was to increase resilience within individuals, teams and the entire organisation. Half-way through the coaching session and wondering what to do with the client's information gathered thus far, Ken asked her to write on three pieces of paper her answers to the question: Where are the fragility, the robustness and the growth in your team given the environment in which the team is working? She duly obliged.

In response to Ken's, *Place each of those pieces of paper where it needs to go*, she laid them out on a large meeting room table.

Now find a place which knows something else about all of that.

She labelled the space, "Overview".

And what do you know here?

Ken was working against time and he also wanted to acknowledge the manager's interest in creativity:

Now find another space in the room where there is creativity.

What kind of creativity is this?

And when creativity is like that, what do you know now about all of that *[gesturing generally at her three pieces of paper]***?**

When the explorer returned to Overview there was a new understanding about what she wanted and needed to do next, and a greater appreciation of the positive features in the system and her capacity for using them.

Ken says,

I guess the learning for me was that, even though I introduced a model (the fragile-robust-growth spectrum) into the explorer's thinking, it was consistent with Clean Space because it continued the self-modelling the explorer had been working through before I introduced it. Apart from the labels for the three pieces of paper and the creativity space I did not add in anything else.

This example illustrates how a little Clean Space can sometimes go a long way.

Importing Clean Space into Other Methods

SYMPTOM
CAUSE
OUTCOME
RESOURCES
EFFECTS
S.C.O.R.E. Model -
Robert Dilts & Todd Epstein

SYMPTOM
CAUSE
OUTCOME
RESOURCES
EFFECTS
S.C.O.R.E. Model -
Robert Dilts & Todd Epstein

SPIRITUAL
IDENTITY
BELIEFS AND VALUES
CAPABILITIES
BEHAVIOURS
ENVIRONMENT
Neurological Levels - Robert Dilts

FIRST POSITION (Self)
SECOND POSITION (Other)
THIRD POSITION (Observer)
FOURTH POSITION (System)
Perceptual Positions

Some of the examples in this chapter retain the Clean Space format and add in features from elsewhere. The following examples do the opposite. Clean Space questions and directions are imported into another process. Almost any process that already makes use of space can benefit from applying some Clean Space principles and features.

Many NLP activities are easily adaptable, especially those championed by Robert Dilts and his colleagues. Those that use perceptual positions, timelines and Neurological Levels are all prime candidates. Chris de Graal took Robert through his own SCORE model using the principles of Clean Space. Chris had Robert sound his responses rather than speaking them, Robert was surprised to find he did not place the C-S-R-O-E spaces on a straight timeline, as is customary. Instead it curved – and the curve had symbolic significance for him.

If nothing else, the simple act of inviting the explorer, rather than the facilitator, to locate each of the spaces can make an important contribution. Adding in some of the Clean Space questions and directions will give the client even more freedom to personalise the process.

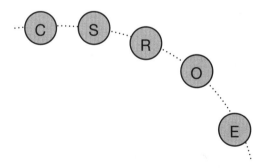

Robert's timeline turned out to be curved

Case Study 10:
Not Too Big for My Boots

A particularly good example of making use of Clean Space questions and directions within another format is Lynne Burney's 'Clean Constellations'. It is based on Family Constellations developed by Bert Hellinger and a similar process used in organisations: Systemic Constellations. Lynne ran a conference workshop showing how she had adapted the Constellations process to include Clean Space principles and features.

Marian joined the session and volunteered to be the seeker (explorer) for a demonstration. She chose as her topic, "I don't want to be too big for my boots." Instead of finding spaces for different aspects of the topic as she would have done in Clean Space, she was instructed to choose people from the group who could represent the various aspects and to move them (by gently guiding them from behind) to appropriate places.

She chose people to stand in as: 'myself', 'too big' and 'boots'. Everyone was silent while they attuned themselves to Marian's constellation.

Marian observed while Lynne used Clean Space questions to ask each of the representatives what they knew from where they were, and what they knew about the other two spaces. They were to report whatever intuitive impressions, feelings and sensations they were experiencing as a representative. Obviously they didn't have much information to go on: Marian's statement of the topic, a short explanation she had given in the beginning and the spatial relationships she had set up. Nevertheless, the representatives seemed to know things that were pertinent to Marian's topic. Unlike traditional Family Constellations, Lynne made no observations, interpretations or suggestions throughout the process.

Lynne asked Marian if she wanted to move the people and add further representatives into the constellation. Marian realised she hadn't created a desired outcome for the session and when she couldn't think of one, she simply chose a man to represent 'desired outcome'. Lynne invited each representative to say what they now knew, ending with Desired Outcome.

Marian was very surprised when he said his impression was like being a strong oak tree; in a previous piece of work some years before she'd had a similar experience – not knowing a desired outcome and choosing a tree to represent it.

After another iteration, during which more representatives were added to the scene, Lynne invited the audience to sit in small groups and reflect on what was happening (while Marian and the representatives stayed where they were). Amidst the general hubbub in the room Marian overheard a colleague, Michael Mallows, say that he thought 'love' was missing from the scene.

When the session recommenced Marian asked Michael to represent 'love'. The representatives were then invited to move to where they intuited they should now be. As you might expect, the presence of love transformed the whole scene.

Lynne then invited Marian to take the place of the person who had been representing 'myself' in the constellation.

Marian said that she felt that somehow the constellation contained her information, even though most of the people taking part were previously unknown to her. She found it a deeply moving experience.

Afterwards, several audience members said that their feet were tingling – which seemed significant given Marian's topic!

I don't want to be too big for my boots.

OTHER WAYS TO USE CLEAN SPACE

People have found some remarkable ways to vary the basic format including using all sorts of things as place holders, a range of methods to locate spaces and move around the network.

Different things to use as space markers

○ Photographs

○ Self-created sculptures

○ Objects which symbolise the spaces

○ People

Ways to locate spaces

○ Random (e.g. use dice to decide how many steps to take in which direction)

○ Divining rod

○ Blindfolded

○ Someone else decides for the explorer

○ Let a horse decide

○ Use the environment (chairs, stairs, balcony, flowerbeds, trees, paths etc.)

○ A fixed structure e.g. a labyrinth

Ways to move around

○ On horseback

○ A fairground gyroscope (known as the Whirligig)

○ All in the mind

Other ideas

○ No words – silently or, optionally, using gesture, dance, voice, musical instrument

○ All in metaphor

To give you a sense of the variety of other ways to use Clean Space, we've selected four examples:

➤ Equine Assistance

➤ The Whirligig

➤ Guided Inner Clean Space

➤ D.I.Y. Clean Space: Facilitating Yourself

Equine Assistance

People in the equine-assisted therapy, coaching and learning fields have incorporated both traditional Clean Language and Clean Space into their work.

One approach has been to conduct Clean Space in a paddock, allowing a horse to move freely. How the horse interacts with the explorer and their space is incorporated into the process. Including the horse in this way is akin to utilising synchronistic events as described on pages 120–121.

Equine masseur and psychotherapist Jeni Edge says:

> Depending on the horse and their sensitivities, they may connect with and play a part in a person's metaphor as they are working with it – but sometimes they take no interest at all. What I've noticed working with Clean Space around horses is that they often come over and take an interest in the person who is working on their stuff when they reach a point of clarification – they seem to sense the shift in that person and are drawn to it.

The method can be extended so that wherever the horse positions itself can become the location of the explorer's next space.

Another method has the explorer creating and moving around their network while riding a horse. One possibility is to allow the horse to 'choose' the location of the spaces (e.g. wherever the horse happens to stop). Its spontaneous movements, such as turning, can also be included (see page 160).

The Whirligig

David Grove wasn't content for people to explore space by walking around a room with the occasional foray onto a chair or turning through 360 degrees. He experimented with several prototypes that allowed people to move with 'six degrees of freedom' – forwards and back, up and down, side to side.

David finally achieved his dream in 2004 when he modified a fairground gyroscope he nicknamed 'the whirligig'. It is still in use today. It has three steel rings, each of which can be rotated on its own axis to allow the explorer to face in any direction. The device is mounted on a trailer and can be towed to various events. It is now owned and operated by Shaun Hotchkiss who helped finance many of David's wild ideas.

The explorer sits at the centre of the rig, securely strapped to the seat and suspended in space. David, accompanied by an assistant, operated the whirligig with extreme sensitivity since even a fraction of a degree one way or the other can make all the difference to the explorer.

The explorer is slowly moved until they find a position where they intuitively know they need to be or their body registers a 'felt sense' about which they may have little cognitive understanding. Minute adjustments of the rig follow until the explorer finds just the right angle, height and direction. After a few Clean Space questions the process repeats.

The effect of being in the whirligig is hard to describe since it is less about language and more about movement, physical sensations and intuitive knowings. Perhaps best to let an explorer, Judy Rees, describe her experience of being in the whirligig:

Judy's Whirligig Experience

A particular orientation reminded me of the day after the London bombings when, in a spirit of "feel the fear and do it anyway" I had been dropped from a crane into a cargo net: 'scad diving'. My body seemed to remember the whole jumble of emotions I'd felt at that time, all the fear and panic and stress of the previous day.

From there I was rotated into various other positions – upside down forwards, upside down backwards, looking out at the stars – before eventually being manoeuvred back to that 'scad diving' position.

Wow, what a difference! This time I was filled with excitement and exhilaration, whooping with joy.

And once released from the device there was a peace, quietness, a sense of, "You don't have to do anything."

Shaun Hotchkiss and David Grove operating the Whirligig

Case Study 11: All in the Mind

The idea for Inner Clean Space came to Sue Charman while she was travelling by train to attend a Clean Space workshop we were running. We had sent an activity similar to the one on pages 16–20 to the participants beforehand. Sue found herself in a packed carriage without the space she needed to do the exercise. She wondered what would happen if, instead of physically moving to different spaces, she moved her mind to different places. Here is her account:

Sitting in the train, I wrote down my topic: "Why do I sometimes think I am not enough?" I stuck it on the flap-down tray on the seat back in front of me so that it was directly ahead of me and I closed my eyes, allowing my thoughts and feelings to run freely over the topic.

Then I silently instructed myself to place myself where I am now in relation to 'being enough'. In my imagination, but not physically, I 'moved' to the right. I discovered that I disappoint myself: I don't meet my own high standards, which it seems are non-negotiable.

I opened my eyes to write this down and then closed them again and found another space, this time very much on the left-hand side. Here I encountered anxiety about what might come out if I opened my mouth because of all the feelings that surge around inside me. I wrote this down.

Finally I went to a third space to record my learnings from the exercise. I was central but further back than at the beginning. I wrote that I have polarised views of myself and that this is confusing and tiring.

Moving to these spaces in my head made a huge difference to how I felt and thought. In the second space a different part of me, one that rarely gets first shout, was allowed to speak.

It had a very different voice: "I am tired of the right-hand space voice, forever demanding excellence and never satisfied." Although anxious, the left-hand space has much more potential for new beginnings and creativity.

The activity allowed me to think and feel differently and this seemed a useful strategy for breaking through old patterns. The work carried on into my dream life that night. All this from a two-minute exercise on a train!

During the course, we offered participants the chance to 'get creative with Clean Space' and Sue worked with two participants to further develop her idea. Their feedback helped her create an inner Clean Space process where an explorer with their eyes closed is guided to move around a network of spaces in their mind.

Guided Inner Clean Space

And find a place where you would like to do this activity.

Write or draw your desired outcome or topic of interest.

And physically place it where it needs it to be.

And return to your seat and close your eyes.

And bring to mind what is on your paper.
[Allow time for them to do this.]

And what do you know here about that topic?

And is there anything else you know here?

And what could this place be called?

The explorer does not write anything down; instead they call out the name of the place and the facilitator keeps a note of the names. To establish a second space, the facilitator continues with:

And in your mind, go to a place that knows something else about that topic.

And what do you know in this place about that topic?

And is there anything else you know in this place?

And what could this place be called?

The process continues with invitations to go to subsequent places and to relate them to one another, referring to the places by name to keep them in mind. Depending on time, establish between three and six places.

To finish the session:

And return to where you are in this room and consider all that you now know.
[Pause.]

And take a deep breath and open your eyes and look at your topic on the paper.

[When eyes are open...] **And what difference does knowing all this make?**

Note the use of 'place' instead of 'space'. When Sue was experimenting with her fellow participants, they found the word 'space' a bit odd in this context and reported that it confined their thinking. Using 'place' however opened up all kinds of possibilities including explorers visiting a meadow, outer space, 'all around my body' and 'my uncle's living room' – all places that could not have been visited in a traditional Clean Space session or, in some cases, in real life.

D.I.Y. Clean Space: Facilitating Yourself

The activity at the front of this book (pages 16–20) was designed for you to experience the fundamentals of Clean Space.

Despite there being no one facilitating, most people get a lot from this very simple process. How else might Clean Space be used when there is no facilitator available?

People have devised a variety of ways to facilitate themselves to valuable insights, learnings and creativity. For example, the essential questions and directions on page 59 can be put on cards and after the start routine has been completed, the explorer turns over a card and asks him or herself the question or follows the direction. A creative twist is to shuffle the cards and pick them randomly.

Another idea is to record yourself giving the directions and asking the questions with appropriate pauses for them to be carried out.

Afterwards you can play back the recording and follow the instructions as an explorer. If you need more control over the gaps between instructions, a portable audio player can be stopped and started as and when you are ready. It's a little like following the audio guides given out by museums and art galleries these days.

Choosing new offices

The three founders of the Dutch consultancy, Gewoon aan de slag, personalised Clean Space to help them choose new offices. First they decided on the six most important criteria for their new offices, "ambience", "readiness to move in", etc. Then a property agent took them to several prospective offices for rent. At each premises they asked the agent to sit down and ignore what they were about to do.

They located a space for each of the criteria and together stood in those spaces, saying what they knew there. No decision was taken or conclusion sought.

When they had visited all the properties they returned to their current offices and established a space for each of the premises. After standing in each one they found a decision space separate from the spaces representing the premises. When they stood here they said, "Choosing was easy. In fact there was no decision; it was obvious to all of us which office was best."

Case Study 12: Chapters in our Book

When we needed to clarify our thinking or to generate new ideas for this book, we naturally turned to Clean Space to assist our own creative process. For example, we used Clean Space to think about the order of our chapters and how the book would flow.

We started by writing the name of each potential chapter on a piece of paper and arranging these around the room. We both found a place to stand and we took it in turns to speak from our respective spaces.

It wasn't long before we were moving to the various chapter headings, talking about what we knew there and asking each other what we knew about the other spaces.

Different metaphors for the possible book structure emerged...

Would it be like a spiral?

Or maybe a hub with a number of spokes?

Or perhaps an ogee?

The fact that there were two of us meant that as well as learning more about our different ideas for the book structure, we were also finding out about how our writing relationship would work. For example, when Marian remarked that it seemed James had been doing a lot of adapting to her ideas, James said he was doing so on behalf of the book. "I want this book to be a good book and I don't mind if it's my idea or your idea of a book. I know my ideas are going to be in there somewhere."

In under an hour, we not only had lots of new ideas about how the book could be structured, we also had much greater clarity about ways we could work together. We had utilised the general features of Clean Space to create the conditions for our own creativity to emerge.

Just as the mind emerges from the actions of individual neurons and their cooperation, the success of an organisation emerges not only from its individual participants, but also from the interplay between them.

JUSTIN ROSENSTEIN

Chapter 7

Group Clean Space

The Purpose of Group Clean Space

We can think of an individual as a system which comprises many interacting subsystems. For example we use emotional and psychological systems to perceive, learn, plan, dream, stay motivated and so on. Each subsystem helps us function at our best, and no part can control the whole. Within a Clean Space session any subsystem may claim a space and provide information relevant to the topic in hand. Then, as the spaces become networked, the interactions between the information produce new, creative and emergent knowledge.

Something similar applies to a group of individuals, whether that is a couple, family, team, department or organisation. If a group is viewed as a system then each individual is a subsystem, and they each bring with them their own perceptions, emotions, ideas, etc. which together create the collective.

The purpose of Group Clean Space is first to reveal and release knowledge held by individuals so that it is available to all, and then to enrich that knowledge by identifying connections, tensions and synergies resulting in a new group awareness. The complexity of a knowledge network grows as new items, places and links are added; eventually a new simplicity surfaces (often in the form of metaphor) which reconfigures the information into insights, solutions and plans.

Group Clean Space is based on the same principles as the individual process, and yet it has some unique features. Rather than running several one-to-one processes simultaneously, the whole group becomes "the explorer" with everyone contributing; it is about collective learning embodied in individual group members.

Just as Clean Space with individuals can be combined with other processes, so can Group Clean Space. For instance, people have successfully combined it with Amy and Arny Mindell's large group process, Worldwork.

Some day, someone will likely write a whole book devoted to Group Clean Space but for now we'll take you on a tour of a few innovative ways conventional Clean Space has been adapted. At the end we provide a comparative summary table that should enable you to modify the process to fit the characteristics of the particular group you are facilitating.

What's Different? What's the Same?

The same principles that guide the facilitation of an individual, guide the facilitation of a group:

- ○ Make minimal interventions
- ○ Keep the process going
- ○ Utilise what happens
- ○ Incorporate spatial metaphors
- ○ Calibrate and respond to psychoactivity
- ○ Keep up with changes in perceptions
- ○ Respect the spaces, spatial metaphors and whole network as if they really exist
- ○ Do not comment on what is happening
- ○ Remember that change and learning occur as a result of the 'group mind' reorganising itself — not from your interventions.

It isn't possible to generate a standard format for a group process because so much is dependent on what it is being used for and the many decisions that have to be made in the moment. Instead we describe examples with a range of groups which illustrate the principles and include a number of variations.

Although there's no standard format, you'll notice that the examples follow a similar flow to the individual version:

1. Preparation and start
2. Establish spaces
3. Establish links, clusters & additional spaces
4. Consider network as a whole
5. Finish

Before anyone steps into a Group Clean Space process you will need to design a framework which takes into account the following:

- ➤ Kind of group
- ➤ Topic and purpose
- ➤ Size of group
- ➤ Space available
- ➤ Time available
- ➤ Set up of the activity.

After reviewing these subjects, we look at working with couples before describing four case studies using Clean Space with groups ranging from 6 to 80 people.

Kind of Group

As you design a Group Clean Space activity, you'll need to bear in mind the kind of group you'll be facilitating. Is it:

One-off? A set of individuals who have come together for a single event, such as a workshop or conference, and who will not meet as a group again.

Ongoing? A group that is already formed and will continue to interact as a group afterwards, such as a family, a project team or a group of colleagues.

Forming? People who have come together for the first time to form a group that will then be ongoing.

Disbanding? A group that has been working together and who are now meeting for a review before going their separate ways.

With an ongoing or forming group, you'll want to consider how the process will support collaboration and collective decisions, or possibly take into account any conflict in the group.

With a one-off or disbanding group, individual learnings are likely to be more important.

Now you are thinking about group work, you may recall that we have already described a couple of ways to use Clean Space with different kinds of groups:

➤ The three owners of a small **ongoing** business using Clean Space to decide on new offices (page 200)

➤ Our self-facilitated **forming** exploration of writing this book (page 201)

Topic and Purpose

In the individual process you simply hand the explorer a piece of paper and they write or draw what they want to make the focus of the session. But with two or more people there first needs to be agreement about the overall purpose for the activity. Who decides and how the topic is to be generated are other factors to consider.

Group Clean Space has been used for a large range of purposes, for example to:

○ Review learning on a training or the progress of a project

○ Explore and resolve a current problem or conflict

○ Generate new and creative ideas

○ Gather or share information

○ Make a decision

○ Organise large amounts of information

○ Envision, as in business visioning and planning, or designing a book.

The topic can be decided in a variety of ways:

○ Each participant choses an individual focus

○ The group creates a joint topic

○ The facilitator sets the topic (e.g. on a training course)

○ The purpose is predefined (e.g. by management or government regulation)

If a couple or a small team want to explore an issue they have spent time considering, they may already have an idea how to represent it. You can start in the usual way, asking them to place their representation where it needs to be. Surprisingly, even in large groups, the position, angle or height of the paper may be altered, but generally it doesn't take very long for a group to place the topic.

Sometimes a group has had the topic given to them and they only need to decide how to represent it. At other times, a group has their own general purpose but does not have an agreed topic. In this case, you can start by using a Group Clean Space process to help them decide, so that 'What is the topic?' *is* the topic. Then run the process again with the agreed subject matter.

If for any reason there is more than one topic, each will need to be represented and located by the group.

We often use Group Clean Space to help people review and consolidate what they have learned during a workshop or other training event. In this case, the topic does not belong to the explorer but to us as trainers, and it is our job to explain it to the group as part of the set up (see Case Study 13).

Size of Group

And what do you know here?

The process you'll design for two or three people is likely to be quite different to the one for 15 or 20. While it might be possible for a few people to stand together in each of six spaces and talk about what they know there, this is unlikely to work in a larger group. The larger the group the more you will need to think about how to keep everyone actively engaged. There are several ways you can do this. You can invite people to:

○ Generate a number of ideas and put each onto separate pieces of paper or Post-its before they start engaging with the space (Case Studies 13, 14 and 15)

○ Walk around the network looking at what's been written, adding to the writing or spaces (Case Studies 13 and 14)

○ Get together as a group in an observer space and call out what they know from there (Case Studies 14 and 15)

○ If there is a very large group, each subgroup can choose a 'representative' who periodically liaises with them (Case Study 16).

Space, Time and Set Up

The Space

Beyond knowing about the group and the topic, another major consideration when designing Group Clean Space is: How will you utilise the available space so that there is some kind of congruence with the activity, while still keeping it as clean as it can be?

For example:

○ Will the main network be restricted to a particular part of the room, and if so what will signify the boundary?

○ Where will people who are temporarily not active in the main network be positioned?

○ Clean Space with groups often involves everyone going to an outside or observer space, does this need to be located in advance?

Amount of Time

While one-to-one Clean Space generally takes between 30 and 60 minutes, it is possible for a group process to last anything from an hour to half a day. Even in a short activity you will need to keep it moving and the longer it goes on the more individuals will need to be kept engaged. One way to do this is to divide the process into a number of discrete steps, where each step sets up the next. In Case Study 16, Group Clean Space is the middle of three clean activities.

The Set Up

Group Clean Space is unusual and you may need to explain some of the principles, structures and processes in advance. For instance, if participants need to create information on paper or Post-its prior to creating the network, the kind of information required will need explaining. Stay as clean as possible. Your aim is to provide the group with just enough information to give them an idea of how the process works, while putting in as few of your own thoughts about what the group should do and how they should respond to your questions and directions. This will be made easier the more you attend to behaviour and process and the less you explain or try to predict the outcome. You will invariably use metaphor. You can either use 'neutral' metaphors or give people a few that make the same point so they have a choice about which one to relate to, resonate or connect with.

Working with Couples

A 'couple' can be any two people in a relationship, whether that is romantic, family, friends, business or otherwise.

When using Clean Space with couples, there are a number of ways to establish the network:

- Each person creates their own independent network (which can be left separate or become connected)
- One person creates a network which the other partner utilises
- The couple creates a joint network like the example in Case Study 12.

Independent networks

If each partner does nothing but watch the other go through a Clean Space process it can have a profound effect. Additionally, each person's network acts as an external map of their perception of the relationship. The spatial organisation simplifies complicated and enmeshed issues. Since the experiences can be referred to 'over there' this depersonalises problems, making it easier for the parties to discuss without triggering old and unproductive reactions.

If the couple does not have a clear idea of what they want, we suggest they start with one of the following topics:

- The relationship
- The kind of relationship I/we would like
- Relating at our best is like...

Utilising another's network

The wife of a couple Penny Tompkins and James worked with felt her husband never really listened, heard or understood her. The husband said that after years of trying to understand his wife, he had accepted he didn't know how to. He was at his wits' end, doubting whether it was even possible for his wife to feel understood.

Penny invited the wife to create a network in the usual way. However, after she established each space the husband was invited to stand in the space and faithfully replicate his wife's experience. With some support from James he began to realise that the easiest way was simply to use as many of his wife's words as he could remember and in particular to preserve her metaphors. He discovered how much he converted his wife's experience into his own way of thinking and felt compelled to solve her difficulties for her.

He located a space for this habit which enabled him to physically and metaphorically separate his own from his wife's experience.

Towards the end of the session we invited him to return to some of his wife's spaces and second-guess what his wife would say when she revisited them. Of course he never got it quite right, but he got near enough on a few occasions to surprise his wife. Now they both knew it was possible for her to feel understood.

Joint network

Couples who create a network together can either agree a joint topic or desired outcome or if they cannot agree, they can each have a topic. The network is built by each of them contributing one space at a time. Alternatively one partner starts and the other adds to the network when they want to.

As in the previous example, things get really interesting when couples visit and relate to each other's spaces. To preserve the additive nature of Clean Space, if a person disagrees or argues with a space created by their partner, they must do that from a new space. Similarly, they cannot move, remove or destroy a space created by the other – without the other's permission.

Sometimes the facilitator needs to intervene to keep the couple describing their in-the-moment experience rather than picking at old wounds, for instance by inviting the couple to find a space for the wound.

Where possible, aim for one idea per space. If one explorer goes from idea to idea, facilitate them to find and name a space for each idea.

You can also invite couples to establish spaces and links for known aspects which have yet to make an appearance. For example, a divorcing couple had not created spaces for their two children until invited to do so. And later they were invited to:

Each find a space for the relationship you would like to have after you are divorced.

And from that space:

And what do you know here about the relationship with your children after the divorce?

We now move on to four case studies about facilitating larger groups.

> Consolidating learning

> Co-inspiring one another

> Endings and new beginnings

> Co-creating with nature, as a collective

Case Study 13: Consolidating Learning

Kind of group:	**One-off or Ongoing learning group**
Topic:	**Review and consolidate learning**
No. people:	**6-12**
Time available:	**60-90 minutes**

This example illustrates one way to facilitate a training group to reflect on and consolidate what they have learned. There are many topics that could be substituted for 'learning' such as: 'reflections', 'benefits', 'take-homes', 'actions' etc.

We have run similar activities several times and what follows is a composite format which can easily be adapted to suit the circumstances. It uses location to *cluster* similar ideas near to one another and dissimilar ideas some distance apart. As people take part in this clustering process, they see others have similar ideas *and* there are things they have not considered. This helps to create a collaborative atmosphere and allows for individual ideas to become part of a group knowing. As the clusters form, people become less interested in 'owning' their individual ideas (e.g. thinking "my Post-it is there"); instead they start to think about how to get the most out of the activity.

1. Preparation

Participants review their notes, the course syllabus and manual. They write their learnings on Post-its or sheets of paper – one learning per sheet.

We often limit this step to the top three to six learnings, depending on the number of people and the time available.

2. Establish Spaces

2a. Ask, *Would someone place one of their learnings where it needs to be [gesture around the space].* Followed by, *And what is this learning called?* and, *And what do you know about [name of learning]?* Then indicate to that person that they can return to their seat.

2b. Ask, *Who has a similar learning?* Invite them to place their Post-it near to the initial one and to name it. If the group is small and you have time you can also ask whether there anything else they know about this learning.

Continue with *Who else has something similar?* and invite them to place and name it.

2c. When there are no more similar learnings, ask, *Who has a different learning?* Invite them to place their Post-it elsewhere, name it and say what they know about it.

The activity is not a 'thematic analysis' (although Clean Space can be used for that); the aim is for participants to enhance their reflections and think about learnings they had not considered.

Repeat steps 2b and 2c. After a few repetitions, the group will get the idea and continue on their own, placing, naming and sorting the Post-its into clusters of learnings.

Up to this point, we actively assist the process with questions and directions; now we step back as the group takes ownership of the spaces and structures that are forming.

3. Establish Links and Clusters

3a. Once all the Post-it notes have been placed and clusters have formed, invite everyone to walk round the network to consider the arrangement of Post-its and clusters and to rearrange them as they see fit.

During this step, someone in the group may pick up a whole pile of Post-its and move it to join another one, or perhaps they'll break one pile into two. They are using the space to structure their ideas, and they are doing it themselves.

3b. When the group seems to have completed 3a, invite everyone to, *Select a cluster and go to it.*

3c. Ask each participant: *And what could this space be called?* (If necessary, you can add, *And what are all these learnings an example of?*)

3d. When everyone has named their cluster, ask, *And what do you know here about one of the other learnings?*

This encourages participants to notice connections.

If there's time, invite people to go to and name the unoccupied clusters and repeat steps 3c and 3d.

Looking into the well of learning.

4. Consider Network as a Whole

No matter how much arranging and linking takes place, leave enough time for the group to consider the network as a whole. Has a structure and logic emerged without anyone designing it that way?

Instruct everyone to, *Find a space outside of all these learnings.* Then ask:

And what do you know here?

And all this *[gesture around the network]* **is like what?**

And what difference does knowing all this make?

During one of these sessions, a participant said that seeing all the Post-its from the outside was like, "Looking into the well of learning"; another described it as like "a flower of knowledge", and another thought it was like "a half-moon, hiding as much as it showed".

5. Finish

Invite people to collect their own Post-its.

Case Study 14: Co-Inspiring One Another

<table>
<tr><td>Kind of group:</td><td>Ongoing (A department who had come together for a day of reflection and professional development)</td></tr>
<tr><td>Topic:</td><td>Co-inspiring one another</td></tr>
<tr><td>No. people:</td><td>14</td></tr>
<tr><td>Time available:</td><td>90 minutes excluding debrief (The Clean Space activity was the last of the day.)</td></tr>
</table>

The topic was previously agreed by members of the department who felt they were missing ways to support each other when working on separate projects. James led this activity with assistance from John Martin, coordinator of the professional development day.

1. Preparation and Start

1a. James and John drew on the work of Humberto Maturana and Pille Bunnell to introduce the idea of 'co-inspiration':

> Co-inspiring happens when two or more people discuss their own projects, interests and reflections in a way that supports each person to gain from the conversation. It is cooperative but it is not a collaboration because there is no joint project.

A brief discussion clarified the purpose of the activity: co-inspiring one another.

1b. Participants wrote or drew their ideas, experience or desires on sheets of paper.

1c. James indicated the space available for the activity (8 x 4 metres). He wrote 'CO-INSPIRING' on a large sheet of paper and invited the group to *Place this where it needs to be.*

Using a large sheet of paper like this keeps the purpose of the activity clearly visible.

> One person placed it on the floor in the middle of the room. Someone else slightly adjusted its position and that seemed OK for the group.

Placing the topic requires someone to make a decision. Others may have a response to that placement or subsequent adjustments. However, acceptance (even tacitly) involves the group in the process.

1d. We strive to design our activities so they are congruent with the group in the 'real' world. Since they were already a department James asked them to create one group 'Observer' space where people could go at any time to reflect on the process and the network of experiences being created. The whole group started in this observer space.

2. Establish Spaces

2a. Individually participants placed one of their sheets in the space in relation to the topic and others' contributions. They stood in that place, read what was on their sheet (adding an explanation or example if they wished) and then returned to the Observer space.

2b. Spontaneous clustering occurred when sheets representing similar ideas were placed near to each other.

At this point the facilitator needs to stand back as much as possible and let the group manage the process themselves.

3. Establish links and additional spaces

3a. When everyone had placed their sheets, they were all invited to go to a space someone else had created and add what they knew. They were handed pens and paper to record their input.

Depending on time and interest, 3a can be repeated several times.

3b. The group was invited to create extra spaces for information that had yet to be included or to create connections between existing spaces.

More connections, issues, feelings, inspirations were expressed, located and linked in the emerging network. This continued with participants contributing in an ad hoc fashion.

4. Consider network as a whole

When the group reached a natural conclusion, everyone was invited to go to the Observer space where their reflections were documented.

5. Finish

5a. After a break, the group sat around the network. They reflected on their learning and captured the experience of co-inspiring and of being co-inspired.

5b. The configuration and content of the sheets were photographed. A collage of the network was created which was circulated to participants and put on a wall of the departmental coffee area.

Feedback from participants indicated that the exercise fulfilled its purpose of opening up ways for department members to be more supportive of each other's work. It was noted that Clean Space had kept a group of highly individualistic people focused on a mutual purpose. For over an hour the entire group had self-organised to maintain their contributions and discussions within the context of co-inspiring. Given the individuals involved, that was no mean feat.

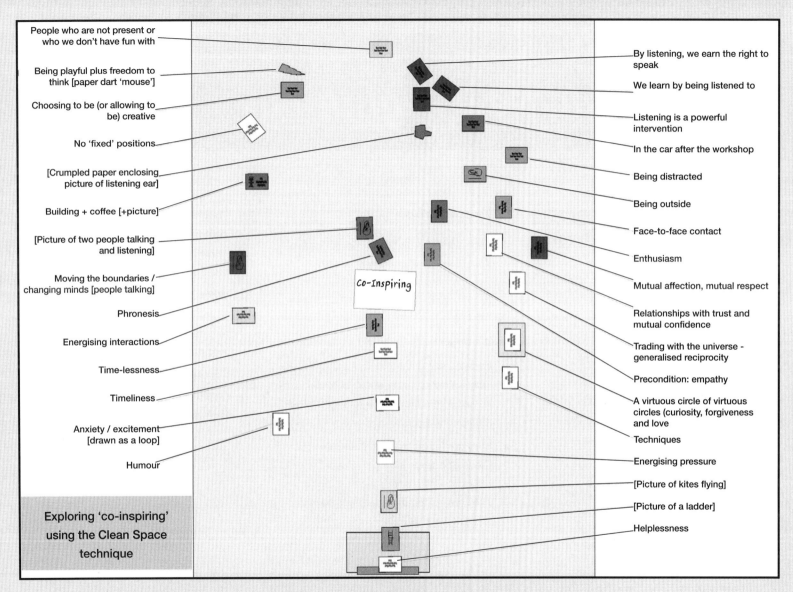

People who are not present or who we don't have fun with

Being playful plus freedom to think [paper dart 'mouse']

Choosing to be (or allowing to be) creative

No 'fixed' positions

[Crumpled paper enclosing picture of listening ear]

Building + coffee [+picture]

[Picture of two people talking and listening]

Moving the boundaries / changing minds [people talking]

Phronesis

Energising interactions

Time-lessness

Timeliness

Anxiety / excitement [drawn as a loop]

Humour

By listening, we earn the right to speak

We learn by being listened to

Listening is a powerful intervention

In the car after the workshop

Being distracted

Being outside

Face-to-face contact

Enthusiasm

Mutual affection, mutual respect

Relationships with trust and mutual confidence

Trading with the universe - generalised reciprocity

Precondition: empathy

A virtuous circle of virtuous circles (curiosity, forgiveness and love

Techniques

Energising pressure

[Picture of kites flying]

[Picture of a ladder]

Helplessness

Co-Inspiring

Exploring 'co-inspiring' using the Clean Space technique

The network showing the location of the spaces at the end of the process.

Case Study 15:
Ending and New Beginnings

Kind of group:	**Disbanding** (a group of volunteers meeting for the last time.)
Topic:	**Ending and new beginnings**
No. people:	**8**
Time available:	**120 minutes**

Within this loose team of volunteers, tensions had arisen during a joint project. The project had been completed successfully and the group came together to celebrate their success and to clear the air for any possible future collaboration. This activity was facilitated by Penny Tompkins and James.

1. Preparation

Each person draws their metaphor for:
The project was like what?

2. Establish Spaces

One at a time:

2a. Each person places their drawing where it needs to be and places him or herself where they are in relation to their metaphor drawing.

2b. They are facilitated with a couple of Clean Space questions to describe what they know here about their metaphor. They are invited to name the space and to mark it with a Post-it.

2c. They return to the group and the next person places their drawing and him or herself in relation to what has already been placed, and is facilitated as in 2b.

2d. When everyone has been facilitated, they all return to the space they created at 2a and each has an opportunity to answer: *And now what do you know here?*

If it seems fruitful and time permits, continue with another round of *And is there anything else you know here?*

3. Establish links and additional spaces

3a. Everyone is invited to do one of the following:

○ Stay in the same place.

○ Go to an existing space and add complementary information (disagreements need a new space).

○ Create a link between existing spaces.

○ Create a new space (named and marked with a Post-it).

3b. Each person is asked :

And what do you know here?

And what does this space know?

Repeat steps 3a and 3b for as long as seems fruitful.

If time is limited you can restrict each person's contribution to a set time (e.g. one minute) signaled by a timer, if necessary.

The more people add to what has been created by others, the more the spaces belong to the group. This makes it easier to go to different spaces, including those they disagree with and find out what they know there.

4. Consider network as a whole

4a. Everyone moves to a collective observer space and reports on their learning/ knowing from there.

4b. Each person then finds their own space that knows something about the network as a whole.

Going first to a group space and then an individual space symbolises the completion of the joint project and people going their own way.

5. Finish

Each person returns to their own starting position at 2a. The group is asked:

And now, what do you know here?

And what difference will knowing this make?

In this particular example, this step was done as a silent reflection after which each person made their own notes. However, in other circumstances an excellent group discussion can follow.

Case Study 16:
Co-Creating with Nature, as a Collective

Kind of group:	**Ongoing** (Members of a spiritual community)
Topic:	**How to co-create with nature, as a collective.**
No. people:	**80**
Time available:	**120 minutes (after the preparatory work)**

This activity was part of a four-afternoon process with 80 members of the Findhorn Spiritual Community in Scotland. Seven clean facilitators were involved in the event. Before we arrived, the community had agreed on a desired outcome: "We intend to clarify/ experience/explore/ground/learn/practise/ how to co-create with nature, as a collective."

This outcome was explored using different clean processes and a variety of group sizes. For the last afternoon we designed and facilitated a three-part activity with Group Clean Space as the middle section.

First we used Caitlin Walker's *Metaphors at Work* process to facilitate departmental teams of 10-12 people to create and draw a joint metaphor for the group outcome. Afterwards, each team chose a representative who would take part in the Clean Space process on their behalf.

Everyone gathered in a large hall. The representatives placed the seven drawings and then they each found a space for themselves. Knowings from these spaces, and other spaces and the links between were identified.

To keep everyone involved, at various intervals the representatives returned to confer with their team who were observing from the sidelines and to change their representative if they wished.

At one point we invited all the observers to come into the space and to place themselves where they were in relation to the drawings and each other. Involving 80 members was the most memorable part of the whole event with people milling about until the movement stopped. Most people were bunched very close together, with a few dotted around the hall outside this cluster.

And what do you know here?

Some people near the centre of the "mass" called it "safe" and "cosy". Others said they had "no space to breathe". Some of those outside the mass said they felt "disconnected"; others on the outer edges said that they were thinking of leaving the community. When we asked, *All this is like what?* a few people made suggestions but when someone said it reminded them of a beehive there was a general murmur of agreement.

The group was invited to *Find where you would like to be.* Slowly the mass began to separate, unwinding into more of a spiral. Some of those on the outside joined the end of the spiral, while a few moved away to the far wall of the hall.

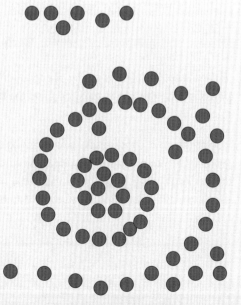

Eventually, when people had found their new place and the group stopped moving, they were asked, *And now, what do you know here?* Some people offered answers and this was followed by, *And what difference does knowing this make, when you intend to co-create with nature as a collective?*

Lastly, the group was invited to take note of what they had learned and after a break they returned to their teams to use another activity to clarify each individual's and each team's next steps.

COMPARING THE CASE STUDIES

There you have it. Four kinds of group, of six to 80 people, each with a different topic in different circumstances.

The table on the right summarises how each group was facilitated through a number of phases:

- ○ Prepare and start
- ○ Establish spaces
- ○ Establish links, clusters and additional spaces
- ○ Consider network as a whole
- ○ Finish.

You can see that there is plenty of scope for varying each of these phases. This enables the process to be tailored to the group and the circumstances within the overall Group Clean Space framework.

One of the main considerations for working with groups is the balance between individual and group experience. All four case studies had some of each; however, both 13 and 15 leant more to the individual while 14 and especially 16 leant toward the group.

	13. Consolidating Learning	14. Co-inspiring One Another	15. Endings and New Beginnings	16. Co-Creating as a Collective
Preparation and Start	Each participant writes/draws their learnings on separate sheets.	Each participant writes/draws their topic-related ideas on separate sheets. Write topic on large sheet of paper and place.	Each participant draws "The project was like what?".	Team metaphors created and placed by representatives. Teams observe from the sidelines.
Establish Spaces	Participants place their learnings one at a time.	Participants place their ideas one at a time.	Each participant locates a space for their metaphor and him or herself.	All representatives locate themselves.
Establish Links, Clusters and Additional Spaces	Clusters form based on similarities and differences. Clusters named and links identified.	Clustering happens spontaneously. Whole group visits spaces created by others, creates links and new spaces.	Whole group visits spaces created by others, creates links and new spaces.	Representatives find other spaces and links between them. Representatives liaise with their team.
Consider Network as a Whole	Whole group walks round and organises network. Participants find own outside observer space.	All go to the group observer space.	All go to group observer space. Individuals find own meta-observer space.	All observers locate themselves in relation to the network. All consider "All this is like what?" Group reorganises to "where you would like to be".
Finish	Collect own Post-it notes.	Network recorded. Group sits around edge of the network and reflections are noted.	Individuals return to their own starting space for silent reflection.	Return to teams to decide next steps.

Around here, we don't look backwards for very long. We keep moving forward, opening up new doors and doing new things, because we're curious... and curiosity keeps leading us down new paths.

WALT DISNEY COMPANY

Chapter 8

And What Difference Does Knowing All This Make?

The Adjacent Possible

We have journeyed in the pages of this book from the essential routines, through the variations needed when certain conditions arise, and via many case studies to arrive at a comprehensive model of Clean Space. We've visited networks, emergence, network effects and psychoactivity. Along the way we've looked at many ways to get creative with the process, including such innovations as Inner Clean Space, Clean Constellations and Group Clean Space.

These ideas grew out of David Grove's earlier work which started with his use of metaphor and symbol inside the body; his later investigation of perceptual space outside the body; and his tireless experimentation following the first Clean Space workshop in 2002. In the last few years before his death in 2008, David further developed his ideas into Emergent Knowledge.

James and Penny Tompkins captured David's ideas when they produced the first formal model of Clean Space in 2003. Since then, they and others have extended it and combined it with other processes.

In writing this book we have added to the sum of knowledge. We have explained and demonstrated:

○ How Clean Space can stand alone, independent of David Grove's other innovations.

○ How to view it as a creativity-generating process.

○ The fundamental features and the essential routines.

○ The importance of network effects and psychoactivity.

○ How to track an explorer's emerging network, calibrate their responses and tailor the process to each individual.

○ How to vary the process to suit a wide range of situations.

○ How to adapt Clean Space for use with groups.

In *Where Good Ideas Come From*, Steven Johnson uses biologist and complex-systems researcher Stuart Kauffman's term, 'the adjacent possible' to explain the creative potential of change and innovation – and its limits. Johnson says:

> The adjacent possible is a kind of shadow future, hovering on the edges of the present state of things, a map of all the ways in which the present can reinvent itself... the world is capable of extraordinary change, but only certain changes can happen.

To explain further, he uses the analogy of a house that expands with each door you open.

In a room with four doors, each leads to a room you've never entered before. When you enter one of those rooms, another three rooms become available to you — three rooms you could not have reached from your original starting place. If you keep opening doors and entering new rooms, who knows where you might end up?

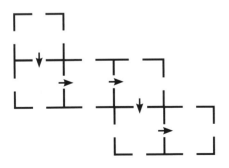

The development of Clean Space diagrammed in this way might look something like this:

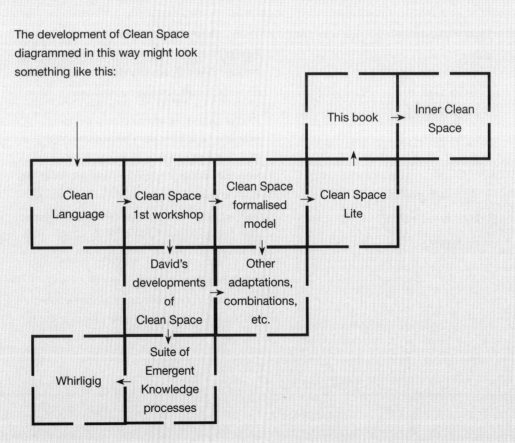

We shall not cease from exploration

And the end of all our exploring

Will be to arrive where we started

And know the place for the first time.

T.S. ELLIOT

Taking what is learned in one room into the next produces a 'ratchet effect' – it builds experience upon experience, knowledge upon knowledge, wisdom upon wisdom.

We have used the notion of the 'adjacent possible' to illustrate the development of Clean Space, and it can also be used as a metaphor for what happens during the process itself. We don't know if David Grove ever came across this term but he certainly embodied the idea in this easy-to-learn and infinitely adaptable process.

As you come to the end of this book, we encourage you to build on the ideas you've found here, and open up some new rooms for yourself.

And it isn't just about going into new rooms. The creative process is also stimulated by returning to previously visited rooms and discovering the world anew. To take just three examples:

○ When a facilitator invites an explorer to return to a space within their network they have the opportunity to accumulate wisdom from that perspective.

○ In writing this book we revisited previous material which enriched and deepened our knowledge and, we hope, produced a rounded account of Clean Space and its various offshoots.

○ As you review the ideas in these pages you will find there is much more to this process than meets the eye and you'll discover even more creative ways to take Clean Space out into the world.

Find an Inner Space...

Let's finish as we started, with a Clean Space activity you can do for yourself. Here is a variation of Sue Charman's Inner Clean Space activity for someone to read to you or for you to record or memorise. We suggest you choose as your topic, "My learnings about Clean Space" or something similar. Later, of course, you can choose any topic you wish.

Before you begin, take a minute or two to write, draw or simply think of a topic.

And when you have done that, place your topic where it needs to be and yourself where you would like to do this activity.

And close your eyes and bring your topic to mind.

And what do you know here about that topic?

And is there anything else you know here?

This is Place 1.

And, in your mind, go to a place that knows something else about that topic.

And what do you know in this place about that topic?

And what do you know in this place about Place 1?

And is there anything else you know in this place?

This is Place 2.

And, in your mind, go to a place that knows something else about that topic.

And what do you know in this place about that topic?

And what do you know in this place about Place 1?

And what do you know in this place about Place 2?

And is there anything else you know in this place?

This is Place 3.

And now, come back to Place 1 in this room.

And consider all you now know about the topic and Place 1 and Place 2 and Place 3.

And take a deep breath and open your eyes.

And what difference does knowing all this make?

And what difference does knowing *that* make?

And what difference does knowing *that* make?

Summary of Clean Space Invitations

The Essential Questions and Directions

Start

Choose topic
- Write or draw your desired outcome or topic of interest.

Locate space
- And place that where it needs to be.
- And place yourself where you are now in relation to that. *[that = topic]*

Know here
- And what do you know here?

Know about there
- And is there anything else you know here about that?

Mark Space
- And what could this space be called?
- And write the name of this space and use the Post-it to mark this space. *(Space 1.)*

Establish Spaces

Locate Space
- And find another space.

Know here
- And what do you know here?

Know about there
- And is there anything else you know here about that?

Mark Space
- And what could this space be called?
- And mark this space *[with Post-it Note]*.

Establish Links

Return to Space
- And return to one of the other spaces.

Update Knowing
- And now what do you know here?

Know about there
- And is there anything else you know here about *[other space]*?

Finish

Return to Space
- And return to *[Space 1]*.

Update Knowing
- And knowing all that *[gesture around the network]* what do you know here now?

Complete
- And what difference does knowing that make?
- When you are ready, collect up your paper and Post-it Notes.

Conditional Questions and Directions

Extended Clean Start

Are you ...

... in the right place?

... at the right distance?

... at the right height?

... at the right angle?

... facing the right direction?

And is that [topic] ...

... in the right place?

... at the right distance?

... at the right height?

... at the right angle?

... facing the right direction?

And is that the right distance between you and that?

Locate Space

- And go to [new space identified by explorer].

- And find a space that represents [where explorer wants to go]. [Proxy Space]

- And find a space that knows about [explorer content].

- And find a space that knows something else about [explorer content].

- And find a space that knows about all of this [gesture around network].

- And find a space outside all of this [gesture around network].

Return to a Space

- And return to [gesture to/ name space].

Know Here

- And is there anything else you know here?

- And what do you know as [gesture to/name pathway of movement]?

- And what do you know from [Proxy Space]?

- And what does this space know?

Know About There

- And what do you know here about [link/group/network]?

- And is there anything else you know here about [Space X] and [Space Y]?

- And what's between [Space X] and [Space Y]?

- And is there anything else this space knows about [topic/space/link/network]?

Update Knowing

- And now what do you know here about [topic/space/ link/group/network]?

Move in Another Direction

Enacting a network metaphor:

- [Direction to enact explorer's active spatial metaphor.]

Turning:

- And turn and face another direction.

- And turn slowly until you are facing another direction.

- And turn in either direction.

- And what do you know in this direction?

Complete

- And where would you like to complete this?

Bibliography

3M, About Post-it® Brand. 3m.co.uk/3M/en_GB/post-it-notes/contact-us/about-us/

Buchard, B., 2012. *The Charge: Activating the 10 Human Drives That Make You Feel Alive.* Simon & Schuster

Csikszentmihalyi, M., 1996. *Creativity: Flow and the Psychology of Discovery and Invention.* Harper Collins

Derks, L., 2005. *Social Panoramas: Changing the Unconscious Landscape with NLP and Psychotherapy.* Crown House Publishing

Dreyfus, H. L. & Dreyfus S. E., 1988. *Mind over Machine: The Power Of Human Intuition and Expertise in the Era of the Computer.* Free Press

Dyson, J., 1997. *Against The Odds: An Autobiography.* Orion Publishing

Frankl, V.E., 1946/1984. *Man's Search for Meaning: An Introduction to Logotherapy.* Touchstone

Geary, J., 2011. *I Is An Other.* Harper Collins

Greenfield, S., 2011. "Outside the Box: The Neuroscience of Creativity" (Video). *The Mind & Its Potential Conference,* Sydney. youtube.com/watch?v=TuTyaBxkWW8

Grove, D., 2002. "Clean Space: The First Workshop." cleanlanguage.co.uk/articles/articles/254/

Grove, D. & Wilson, C. 2005. Emergent Knowledge ΣKTM and Clean Coaching. *The Model,* Edition 2. cleanlanguage.co.uk/articles/articles/47/

Grove, D. & Wilson, C. 2005. Six Degrees of Freedom: Intuitive Problem Solving with Emergent Knowledge. *Resource Magazine.* Edition 5. cleanlanguage.co.uk/articles/articles/44/

Harland, P., 2009. *The Power of Six.* Wayfinder Press

Hotchkiss, S. & Grimsley, C., 2013. "An Introduction to Clean Space" (DVD). NLP in the North West.

Johnson, S., 2011. *Where Good Ideas Come From: The Seven Patterns of Innovation.* Penguin

Karpman, S. B., 2007. "The New Drama Triangles." USATAA/ITAA Conference Lecture August 11, 2007 (PDF). karpmandramatriangle.com/pdf/thenewdramatriangles.pdf

Kolb, D. A., 1984. *Experiential Learning: Experience as the Source of Learning and Development (Vol. 1).* Prentice-Hall

Lakoff, G. & Johnson, M., 1980. *Metaphors We Live By.* The University of Chicago Press

Lawley, J., 2003. "Self-Organising Complex-Adaptive Systems: A Large Group Metaphor Process". cleanlanguage.co.uk/articles/articles/216/

Lawley, J., 2006. When Where Matters: How psychoactive space is created and utilised. *The Model,* January. cleanlanguage.co.uk/articles/articles/29/

Lawley, J., 2007. "The Neurobiology of Space" cleanlanguage.co.uk/articles/articles/196/

Lawley, J., 2011. Joining Up the Work of David Grove. *Acuity* Vol.2, No.1, April cleanlanguage.co.uk/articles/articles/222/

Lawley, J. & Tompkins, P., 2000. *Metaphors in Mind: Transformation Through Symbolic Modelling.* The Developing Company Press

Leung, A. K., Kim, S., Polman, E., Ong, L., Qiu, L., Goncalo, J. A., & Sanchez-Burks, J., 2011. "Embodied Metaphors and Creative 'Acts'." Cornell University, ILR School. digitalcommons.ilr.cornell.edu/articles/486/

Loftus, E., & Palmer, J., 1974. Reconstruction of Auto-Mobile Destruction: An Example of the Interaction Between Language and Memory. *Journal of Verbal Learning and Verbal Behavior,* 13

Luft, J. & Ingham, H., 1955. The Johari Window, A Graphic Model of Interpersonal Awareness. *Proceedings of the Western Training Laboratory in Group Development.* University of California

Martin, S.J., Goldstein, N.J. & Cialdini, R.B., 2014. *The Big Small: Small Changes That Spark Big Influence.* Profile Books

Maturana, H. & Bunnell, P. 2004. Personal communication at the *UK Systems Society Annual Conference*, St Annes College Oxford, 7–8th September 2004

Mindell, A., 1995. *Sitting in the Fire: Large Group Transformation Using Conflict and Diversity.* Lao Tse Press.

Oppezzo, M. & Schwartz, D, 2014. Give Your Ideas Some Legs: The Positive Effect of Walking on Creative Thinking. *Journal of Experimental Psychology: Learning, Memory, and Cognition,* Vol. 40, No. 4

Pinker, S., 1997. *How The Mind Works.* Penguin

Prochaska, J.O., Norcross, J.C. & DiClemente, C.C., 1995. *Changing for Good: A Revolutionary Six-Stage Program for Overcoming Bad Habits and Moving Your Life Positively Forward.* HarperCollins

Tompkins, P. & Lawley, J., 2003. Clean Space: Modeling Human Perception through Emergence. *Anchor Point* Vol. 17, No. 8. cleanlanguage.co.uk/articles/articles/24/

Tompkins, P. & Lawley, J., 2007. "Iteration, Iteration, Iteration". cleanlanguage.co.uk/articles/articles/191/

Tompkins, P. & Lawley, J., 2009. "Clean Space Revisited". cleanlanguage.co.uk/articles/articles/255/

Tosey, P., Sullivan, W. & Meyer, M., 2013. "Clean Sources: Six Metaphors a Minute?" University of Surrey academia.edu/9774145/Clean_Sources_Six_metaphors_a_minute

Tuckman, B. W., 1965. Developmental Sequence in Small Groups. *Psychological Bulletin* Vol. 63, Issue 6

Walker, C., 2014. *From Contempt to Curiosity: Creating the Conditions for Groups to Collaborate using Clean Language and Systemic Modelling.* Clean Publishing

Way, M., 2013. *Clean Approaches for Coaches: How to Create the Conditions for Change using Clean Language and Symbolic Modelling.* Clean Publishing

Wilber, K., 2001. *A Theory of Everything: An Integral Vision for Business, Politics, Science and Spirituality.* Shambala

Books that include Clean Space applications

Campbell G., 2015. *Panning for Your Client's Gold: 12 Lean Clean Language Processes.* Balboa Press

Dunbar, A., 2017. *Clean Coaching: The Insider Guide to Making Change Happen.* Routledge

Harland, P., 2009. *The Power of Six: A Six Part Guide to Self Knowledge.* Wayfinder Press

Wilson, C., 2017. *The Work and Life of David Grove: Clean Language and Emergent Knowledge.* Matador

Index

About the Authors

James and Marian working together

James Lawley gave up his career as a senior manager in a multinational company not knowing what he was going to do with the rest of his life. He retrained in NLP, which enabled him and his wife, Penny Tompkins, to model innovative psychotherapist David Grove. They formalised David's brilliant clean approach and for more than 20 years have continued to develop the field and help extend its application into coaching, education, organisations and more recently research.

James with Penny authored *Metaphors in Mind: Transformation through Symbolic Modelling.* He has also published articles in a number of leading academic journals and there are over 200 of his articles and blogs freely available on cleanlanguage.co.uk.

Marian Way started her working life as a maths teacher and went on to work for Weight Watchers, where she and a colleague developed the Points Diet. She also created and delivered training programmes for people at all levels within the organisation.

When she came across NLP and then Clean Language, Marian transitioned to a third career as a clean coach and trainer. She now delivers training in many of David Grove's clean approaches, as well as Systemic Modelling, a method for using clean with groups devised by her business partner, Caitlin Walker.

Marian is the author of *Clean Approaches for Coaches: How to Create the Conditions for Change using Clean Language and Symbolic Modelling.*